PUSHING THROUGH

Pushing Through is a wonderful and very inspirational book. I knew Rex and cycled with him many times alone and with other teammates while he was formally training for various events. We also spent a good deal of time talking off the bike. I hope this book enjoys a broad global audience, because Rex's story applies to numerous people who have had to work through and overcome incredibly difficult situations

— Marc Bekoff - Renowned Animal Behaviorist

Co-founder / Jane Goodall: Ethologists for the Ethical Treatment of Animals.
Author: Canine Confidential: Why Dogs Do What They Do
Professor Emeritus at University of Colorado, Boulder
marcbekoff.com

INSPIRED BY A TRUE STORY

PUSHING THROUGH

LORI YERXA

INSPIRED BY A TRUE STORY

PUSHING THROUGH

by

LORI YERXA

Book Cover by BJ McCollum
Author Photo by Gerenel Galvez
Polaroid Photo by Jose Alcala
Text copyright © 2019 by Lori Yerxa
ISBN 9781692325015

DEDICATION

This story is dedicated to all those making an
effort to push through everyday
no matter how hard it is.

.

ACKNOWLEDGMENTS

I begin by thanking my cousin, Terri, who upon reading the very first draft said; "let's start with the first paragraph," when she could have justifiably said – maybe writing isn't for you. To all of you who taught me about the world of competitive cycling and shared stories about Rex, my gratitude is overflowing. Thank you, Steve, for sharing the World Ride documentary with me. To my writer's group; Rita, Christine, and Terry, I learned so much from you. Thanks for hanging in there with me. Thank you, Sharon, who told the truth and helped me cross the finish line. Mom, thank you for the final polish and saving me from embarrassment. To my husband, Alan, who never wavered in his support for me on this path of meltdowns and heck yeahs, you are my Favorite! Thank you to all of the people who encouraged me to keep pushing through until –The End. I could not have done this without you. Most of all, thank you to God for challenging me with this assignment. I hope I have served you well.

This work is based on real events.
Certain events, dialogue, and characters
were created for the purpose of
fictionalization.

INSPIRED BY A TRUE STORY

PUSHING THROUGH

LORI YERXA

1

ARKANSAS

"Oh I'd love to be an Oscar Mayer wiener," sang 7-year-old Rex at the top of his lungs, his big smile exposing the brown streaks on his teeth. His brother, Roger, two years older, also sang along with the television. Rex in his Spiderman pajamas and Roger wearing a light blue set, were stomping across the living room floor, like the parade in the commercial. The second they heard the awful vomiting coming from the back bathroom, they stopped, as if they had been touched in a game of freeze tag.

"I hate that noise," Rex whispered.

Roger put his chubby arm around his little brother. "He does it every morning," he said, slowly shaking his head. Roger turned up the volume to the TV then dove onto the couch. "Come on, you can't hear it now."

Rex joined him and they continued watching Wiley E. Coyote and the Roadrunner. Soon, Rex's eyes went to the hallway. He poked Roger in the side to get his attention.

Their father, Lendy, was coming down the hall. He was wiping his mouth with a towel. Rex's body stiffened.

When he reached the living room, their father glanced at the TV, at the boys, then directly at Roger. "Turn that fucking thing down," he said, "or I'll throw it out the window."

Roger ran to the TV and turned it down. Rex sprang up; he could feel the tension between his brother and father as they fixated on each other.

"I'm going outside," Roger announced, not wanting to fight with his dad.

"You better," Lendy said, flinching toward his 9-year-old son, as if he were going to strike him. Lendy watched as Roger ran out to the porch, the screen door slamming behind him, then, slicking back the comb-over hair that had fallen in his face, Lendy turned to little Rex. "What are *you* lookin' at boy?"

Rex shrugged. "Nothing. I'm going outside, too."

As Rex walked toward the door, his dad, reeking of Old Spice, grabbed him by the collar and held Rex tight against his beer gut. The first blow landed on Rex's ear, he winced, and felt overwhelmed by his father's strength.

Lendy, not needing a reason, continued to pummel his son's head and shoulders in rapid-fire motion.

"Mom! Mom!" Rex wailed, frantically wriggling his scrawny body. Pauline was in the back bathroom sorting through her pill bottles, rummaging for her morning uppers. "Mom." The sight of his mother hurrying down the hallway, still in her bathrobe should have brought Rex relief, as Lendy squeezed his son tighter and told him to, "shut up."

"You let him *be*, Lendy!" Pauline screamed, throwing the bottle of pills she was holding at her husband. "He ain't done nothin' to you!"

The distraction caused her husband to loosen his grip, allowing Rex to get a couple of stinging kicks to his dad's shin before escaping out the front door. Rex was brave that way.

From out in the street, Rex and his brother, still wearing their pajamas, watched through the living room window as their mother flailed and threw everything within reach at her husband – magazines, newspapers – anything she could grab.

The commotion of tables being knocked over, lamps shattering, and his mother's pleading cries could be heard all the way to where they stood.

"We should have gone with Lisa to the carnival," Roger said, referring to their older sister. The lump in his throat made it hard to speak.

"Yeah, and never come back." Rex hung his head and kicked the dirt. Another piece of his young soul had broken off and shattered like a melting iceberg hitting the ocean.

Rex and Roger sought refuge under the big shady Maple tree at the edge of the yard, on that muggy, July morning in Fayetteville. They felt safe there, as if the dense canopy of leafy branches could protect them, or that the rushing wind would scoop them up and carry them on invisible wings to a happier land. Hiding behind the thick, knobby trunk, Rex started fantasizing about floating away to a far off kingdom where men weren't drunkards and didn't hit their sons. Ironically, it would be his dad who would make that fanciful wish of floating away come true.

***

One night when Rex was 8, he had a terrible toothache and couldn't sleep. He was trying to be quiet, but his sobbing was loud enough for his father to hear. Irritated, Lendy brought his son a small amount of light brown juice. "Drink it."

"Yes, sir," Rex whimpered. He sat up as Lendy handed the boy a small glass. Rex gulped down the liquid that smelled like a solvent you would sterilize the bathroom with. He tried his best not to gag at the unexpected harsh taste, while his father stood over him and glared, the crease between his eyes deep. Rex gave him back the empty shot glass without saying a word. His father turned and walked out of the room. "Now stop whining," he ordered as he shut the door.

Rex lay back down pulling the covers over his head, feeling small about crying in front of his dad. A few minutes later, his toothache went away and, even though he was awake, he felt as though he were in a dream and his bed was floating around the room.

The next day, Sunday, Rex and Roger were out playing Hit the Target, in the backyard. "I had a toothache last night," Rex said, "and dad brought me some of his whiskey." Rex picked up a smooth, round, gray-colored rock that fit perfectly in between his thumb and forefinger. "Well it was stinky so I think it was moonshine." He tossed the rock two feet up in the

14

air a couple of times before he cocked his arm back and threw the rock as hard as he could at his Folgers coffee can.

"No way! Dad gave you some of his moonshine? He never lets anyone have any."

The boys were with their dad and his buddy once when the men were making moonshine on the friends back patio. Rex and Roger watched that day as the men stirred cornmeal, sugar, and yeast into a large rusting vat full of water. Lendy told them it was barbecue marinade. The boys knew it was alcohol by the odor, even before the older men carried on about the word moonshine, which came from the verb moonshining. Overhearing the conversation that day, the boys learned that moonshining meant activity was being done late at night, by the light of the moon, so nobody would know.

"I can't believe dad gave you some. Maybe I should tell him I have a toothache," Roger went on.

"It tasted terrible, it burned my mouth. Then I felt real funny, in a good way. I want to have some more. Have you ever had any?"

"No. I asked one time why he liked it so much and he told me it was none of my business." Roger whizzed his rock at an empty plastic coolant container.

Rex raised an eyebrow. "Follow me." His predisposition to addiction was already taking control, but like a frog in warming water, he had no idea his troubles were heating up.

The boys tiptoed through the quiet house, careful not to wake their mother, asleep from taking her afternoon Valium. Lendy was at the local tavern and Lisa was in her bedroom doing homework.

"You go first. I'll stand guard," Rex whispered, peaking around the kitchen threshold. "Coast is clear." Roger held the container over the kitchen sink and twisted the cap off of the fullest bottle.

By the end of summer, the boys had developed a habit of sneaking sips out of the bottles that neatly lined the kitchen counter. Some held brown liquids and in others, the liquid was clear, like water. Some were big jugs with handles, others were tall and slender. The different colored labels fascinated Rex. Although he could not read all the words, he knew what was in the bottles – his dream world.

Little Rex no longer thought twice about the gasoline flavor or the acrid smell. Even the moonshine became palatable. He anticipated how the alcohol heated his body and left a burning sensation as the liquid traveled through his insides, down to his stomach. He craved the fuzziness that came over him a few minutes

16

after ingesting alcohol. He wanted to be in that magical world where his body felt airy as if it really could float, and no matter how hard the sadness knocked on his heart, was not allowed in.

2

GRANDMA AND GRANDPA'S

Two years later, Lendy and Pauline divorced. Rex had just turned 10 and plump Roger was now 12. Lendy moved to California for work. Due to her pill habit, Pauline was incapable of taking care of her energetic, wayward sons, so the boys were sent to live with their grandparents on their farm several hours away in the Ozark mountains. Older sister Lisa, stayed to finish school and take care of her mother.

For a while, the structure was good for the boys. They were doing better in school and there wasn't any whiskey to sneak. They were respectful toward their grandparents and always did what they were told. Then, on a sleepy afternoon during spring break, while playing among the trees out by the pond where they swam and fished for trout, everything changed.

"Do you smell something?" asked Roger.

"Weird, it smells like dad's moonshine bottles." Rex put his nose in the air. "Yep, that's what it smells like alright. Let's find it." He sniffed around like a hound dog on a mission, remembering the floating sensation he used to love.

"Over here, I think I found it," Roger called out.

When Rex got closer he saw that the bottom of one of the big pines didn't look right. Sawdust and dirt were piled in the opening where someone had hollowed out the trunk. The boys started digging and came upon a quart of moonshine buried inside.

Roger stared at the dirty jar. "Whoa, is that what I think it is?"

"Moonshine? Go wash it off."

Roger went to rinse off the jar in the pond while Rex kept digging in the soil. He became a burrowing groundhog flinging the dirt in every direction. The boys hit the jackpot, unearthing 10 quarts of moonshine inside that tree trunk.

Rex dusted off his clothes, pried open the lid and, with worn-out arms, knocked back the wet jar, Roger cleaned, and

19

started quaffing. The temperature was rising on his predisposed wiring to addiction and still, he had no idea.

They each downed a few shots, ran back to the house to pack up their sleeping bags, snacks, a kerosene lantern, and some fishing poles and bait. They found grandma in the living room sitting in her lift chair and told her they wanted to sleep by the pond and wake up before dawn to fish while the trout were biting. Grandma agreed, cautioning the boys to be careful in the dark.

Roger nodded in response, his blue eyes twinkling, as he and Rex flew out the door. They ran as fast as they could, hooting and hollering, dodging cow patties across the pasture, their hair flopping up and down with each stride.

They reached their destination in record time and threw together a makeshift camp in a spot that was in their minds close but far enough away to be inconspicuous about their find. The boys hurriedly smoothed out the ground with their hands to remove any twigs or rocks and rolled out the sleeping bags. They hadn't been this excited in a long time.

Rex retrieved the quart he left open by the Pine, and the boys sat facing the pond. A blue heron extended its neck and in a flash plunged its bright orange beak into the water snatching up its dinner. Each time the bird swallowed another minnow, the boys swigged some moonshine.

As the rays of the sun shining on the pond faded away, the boys retreated to their makeshift campsite. The sky was clear and the moon bright, so Roger kept the lantern low. Hours later, the flame flickered and the boys passed out.

The next morning, drenched in sweat, Rex unzipped his sleeping bag and slipped his left leg out. The cool breeze felt good on his hot body. He pushed down the top of the sleeping bag, revealing his bare chest and rolled over to block the bright sunrise from piercing his eyes. "Roger, you awake?" Rex pressed his tongue against the roof of his mouth trying to create saliva in hopes of ridding the awful taste of cottonmouth.

"Yeah, I'm awake, puke boy." Roger threw a clump of dirt at Rex. "Puke boy, puke boy."

"Fuck you, you're making that up."

"It's right there shit-brain."

Rex brushed the fodder off of his sleeping bag and looked over. Sure enough not ten-feet away was a circle of vomit. Rex saw the proof but didn't remember throwing up and lay there stupefied. He was unsettled as he strained for the tiniest bit of information, there was none, as if that piece of time had not elapsed. Even so, it did not keep him from getting sloshed whenever he could for the following six months.

21

When he got home from school one late-spring day, Grandma told him dinner would be later than usual. Rex went out to the barn where he was alone and crawled behind the bales of hay to where he and Roger hid their stash, so it would be closer access, than down by the pond.He leaned back onto a bale of hay, the course alfalfa scratching his neck. When he opened the lid to the last quart of moonshine, the acrid nose-burning turpentine odor snuffed out the aroma of freshly cut feed. He imbibed and sat still as the trail of heat ran through his body and he began to float away into his addiction, relishing in this pain-free world, until he heard his name.

"Rex, where are you boy? It's time for dinner." Grandma waddled her 200 pounds to the side door and yelled for Rex.

"Shere I'm grandzma." Rex ran from the barn, past her and straight to the bathroom, not wanting to be found out.

He washed his hands and splashed water on his face, thinking that would sober him up a bit. He stood up tall and put his shoulders back before leaving the bathroom. As soon as he opened the door, he smelled the pot roast grandma had simmering.

Rex sat down at the table where the others were waiting. "Shmells goot, grand-hut-ma."

"Is there something wrong with you Rex?" Grandma asked.

"No, ma'am. Pleaszh pash the biscuits." Rex noticed Roger had his hand over his mouth covering his laugh.

"Boy, are you OK?"

"Yesh, Grandpa. It's just the allergy medicine." Rex didn't look at Roger this time, fearing he might burst out laughing and they both would get in trouble.

After dinner, Rex and Roger went back out to the barn. Rex held up the last bottle of rotgut. It was only half full. "We're going to have to get some more."

3

THE UNTHINKABLE

One night, after their chores were done, the boys went to hang out in their bedroom. On their way up the stairs, Rex had an idea.

"Let's sneak out and get some whiskey from The Corner Market." Rex quickened his pace up the stairs.

"What? How?" Roger asked as the boys entered the bedroom.

"We can tie our sheets together and scale out the window. I saw it in a movie."

"Are you crazy? That's stupid. We're too high up."

Against his better judgment, Roger went along with the idea. The boys gathered up the dingy plaid sheets on their twin beds and tied the ends together with double knots they learned to make while fishing with their grandpa.

"Here, hold onto this end while I lower it down." Rex hung the sheet out of the window and leaned over the frame with his belly pressed into the sill. "Yep, it reaches with room to spare. Victory!"

Roger bent down and weaved his end of the sheet over and under the bed frame until it was secure. He pushed the bed against the wall under the window so it wouldn't slide while they were scaling down. "Done."

"Good, I'll go first." Rex climbed onto the window ledge, sat and straddled the makeshift rope.

"What if someone sees the sheet?" Roger's heart was already pounding.

"They won't, they're busy watching TV." Rex cautiously peered over the ledge. This time the ground seemed a lot farther away. He let go of the sheet one hand at a time to wipe his sweaty palms on his jeans.

"What are you waiting for? If we're going to do this, go!" Roger lunged toward Rex and faked like he was going to push him.

"Fuck it." Rex gripped the sheet and wrapped his wobbly legs around it like a fireman going down a pole. "See you on the ground."

When it felt safe, Rex let go and jumped the remaining five feet, somersaulting on the landing. He gathered himself then waved his brother on, nervous, as Roger, much bigger, lowered himself in the same way. The boys, high-fived, then vanished into the still night. Uneasiness followed them, like a pair of eyes watching in secret, as they silently trotted down the dirt road on their way to breaking the law.

Once there, Roger surveyed the area to make sure nobody was watching them as they approached the white brick building. Confident they were alone, the boys circled the small market, scouting out the best way to break in.

The windows were too high. They agreed to try the back door first since it was in the dark and mostly out of view.

While his brother fumbled with the doorknob, Rex constantly looked over his shoulder, his heart beating out of his chest. "Hurry up."

"Why don't you shut up and hand me that rock right there?"

"That's too loud, someone is going to hear us."

"Shut the fuck up, will ya?" Roger wiped the sweat from his brow on his shoulder sleeve and smashed the knob with the rock. The door popped open. In that instance, all they could do was stand there, spellbound, staring at each other with their mouths wide open. The adrenaline rush from committing the crime was a thrill in itself.

Oh shit! This is really happening, thought Rex.

Roger went first. They tiptoed around the store as quietly as they could, trying to find the aisle with the booze. Roger stopped abruptly a couple of times causing Rex to bump into him.

"Watch where you're going," griped Roger after Rex chinned him in the shoulder blade.

"You watch where you're going."

"I am watching where I'm going."

"Well, don't stop so fast." Rex rubbed his chin.

"Pay attention."

They both had been in that market many times before and knew the layout, but in the dark stillness they were disoriented and every sound was amplified. Rex could hear himself breathing, as if he were underwater. The ticking of the wall clock made him think an alarm might sound and he would hear sirens in the distance. It was eerie. A shiver ran up his spine. Upon turning a corner, he gasped when he saw the glow of the Budweiser sign and thought it was somebody holding a flashlight.

After bumbling around the store, the brothers happened upon the beverage row. They froze and with their mouths wide open. Finally!

"What should we get?" whispered Rex.

"I don't know, just pick one." The boys stared at the large selection on the shelves.

"Well, which one, the biggest one?"

"I don't care."

"All right then. I'm taking Wild Turkey," Rex snatched the bottle.

"Good, I'm grabbing some Jim Beam."

"Should we swipe more than one?"

"Rex, would you give it a rest? Let's get the hell out of here before we get busted."

They hid the goods under their flannel jackets and hurried to the back door. It creaked as Rex inched it open. He poked his head out and peered around to make sure the coast was clear. Full of adrenaline, they ran a few more blocks down the road, to a secluded spot in the woods, a small clearing in the trees. There was an old weather-worn picnic table in the center of the open space where you could sit underneath the stars.

"Chug it, Chug it," chanted Rex as he watched Roger flip his bottle upside down. Roger gulped as fast as he could, whiskey running down his chin. When he started gagging he tipped his bottle upright and saw that a good bit of the contents was gone. "Your turn." He beat on his chest like King Kong after winning a battle.

"Let me see?" Rex matched his bottle to Rogers. "Shit, I'll beat that."

Rex tipped up his Wild Turkey and guzzled for a full minute, alcohol spilling down his chin and neck, the way it did on his brother. When done, he slammed his bottle down on the table next to Rogers; they consumed an equal amount.

"I thought you were going to- burrrrrrp- me?"

"Braaaaaaaaap. Beat you on that." Rex continued devouring his bourbon.

The brothers howled at the moon and fell down laughing. The evening's rite-of-passage welded in them a shatterproof bond.

An hour later the brothers were sufficiently inebriated. Knowing he had to work with his grandpa in the morning, Roger stashed his bottle in a tree and left. Rex stayed by himself a while longer.

Lying down on top of the table, Rex became engulfed in the silent, peaceful sanctuary: alone in the forest, hidden by the darkness. He was wishing his life could always be this serene as he soaked in a few more minutes of utopia before heading home.

When he was ready to go, he staggered to his feet, kicking over his bottle, and steadied himself on the picnic table until the trees stopped spinning.

Leaving his bottle there, he walked to the avenue, to hitch a ride home. It was around 11:00. After a few minutes, a trucker pulled over and offered him a lift.

"Where ya headed?"

"Down the road a waysszz," Rex slurred, climbing into the large cab.

"Hang tight for a minute," the guy said, "I have to take a piss."

"OK," mumbled Rex.

His eyes followed the seemingly friendly man's hand as he reached down and turned up the stereo. "Radar Love" was playing. The driver hopped out of the truck and started walking, but Rex was too impaired to notice that the man stepped around to his side of the cab. The door on Rex's side burst open and the driver yanked him out of his seat.

Rex squirmed and thrashed as hard as he could, kicking and trying to pry the man's hand loose from his mouth. He was weak and too incoherent to fight as hard as he normally could. The savage dragged him back into the trees. Rex screamed but the sound was muffled.

"Shut up, you little punk," ordered the attacker who was three times Rex's size. "Make a peep and I'll kill you." Terror seared through Rex's spirit.

Rex fought and flailed, but was unable to break free from the man's immobilizing grip. Rex was raped viciously that night and left in the woods like a piece of trash. Unlike a short time earlier, now he lay there limp and abandoned, cloaked in blackness, empty, begging to die.

For hours Rex contemplated not returning home. He couldn't bear to face his family and tell them what had been done to him. He concocted scenarios of running away, each one ending with him miserable and alone. Finally, he passed out until the sunlight streamed through the trees and woke him.

He conceded that he had nowhere else to go, swallowed hard, pulled himself together and began the desolate walk home. His wicked hangover was a welcome distraction from the excruciating physical pain inflicted on him. He tried to pretend the horror he endured in the woods had not occurred, but the visible evidence of scrapes and bruises left by the assault made it impossible.

The psychological torment, however, was worse than the bodily harm. Unwelcome tears burst forth no matter how hard he strained to stifle them. Scared and confused, he decided it would be best to tell. He knew he needed help.

4

TELLING

The house smelled of morning coffee as Rex tiptoed across the living room. He knew his grandma would be in the kitchen fixing breakfast and didn't want to call attention to himself just yet. He hid beside the doorway, concentrating on his grandma scrambling eggs at the avocado-green stove with her back to him, her apron strings falling well below her waist. His breathing barely perceptible, his cheeks hot from streaming tears. He squeezed his eyes shut, hard, trying to shake the emotional residue from what happened just a few hours prior.

When he heard the clomping of boots coming from the side door, he hurried and wiped his face with his soiled T-shirt then walked into the kitchen at the same time Roger and his grandpa entered from the other door. Roger's eyes widened when he saw his little brother. Rex shook his head no, signaling Roger to not say anything.

"Everyone ready to eat?" asked grandma. She turned and saw Rex, battered. Their eyes met and Rex began to sob convulsively. The spatula fell from Grandma's hand spattering bits of grease as it hit the floor. Tears filled her eyes as she witnessed the anguish emanate from Rex's very core. She had never seen her grandson so distraught.

"Rex, my goodness, come, sit down. What's going on?" asked Grandma, compassion in her voice.

"Boy, what happened to ya?" Grandpa also asked.

They all sat down at the Formica table, and Grandma slid the plastic napkin holder to the middle and handed Rex a napkin to wipe the tears and snot dripping down his face.

Roger stayed quiet.

"During the night, I….I, I was walk….there was a man." Rex slid to the edge of the seat where it was less painful to sit.

"Rex, what man? Who is this man?" asked Grandma.

"I d-don't…." Rex's chest heaved as he took in air.

33

"Calm down now boy, it's OK. What happened?" Grandpa wanted to know.

Rex eyed Roger, who was fighting back tears. His face was white and his crinkled forehead made a crease between his eyes.

"I wa...was walking," Rex choked. "A man in a semi stopped and said he would give me a ride home, so I got in."

"What did that man do to you, son?" Grandma asked again.

"H..he yanked me out and... dragged me into the woods." Pellets of distress gushed from Rex's eyes. " I fought as hard as I could. I kicked and tried to get away. His hand was over my mouth." Rex collapsed onto the table, and buried his face in the crook of his arm, his back rising and lowering with each gasp of air. From his peripheral vision, he saw Roger wipe his eyes on his sleeve. A heavy silence lingered.

"Did the man take your pants off?" Grandma finally asked.

"Yes," whispered Rex.

"Grandpa, get the car. We're taking the boy to the emergency room."

Grandma, Grandpa, and Roger slowed their walk to stay with Rex's labored pace. "I don't want to go. I'm going to be alright, I promise." His fearful pleads were met by Grandma's warm hand on his shoulder as they approached the ER entrance.

Sadness and embarrassment pulled down his face, as Rex stood motionless just inside the exam room door. The nurse maneuvered about the room, her short brown hair curled under and tucked behind her ears. The light blue scrubs fit tight across her plump tummy. She paused and smiled at him.

"Hi, Rex, my name is Patty and I'm going to be administering your exam this morning. I'm required to tell you what is going to happen here today. Are you comfortable standing there or would you like to sit down?"

Rex kept his head low. "I'm all right standing." His voice quivered.

"OK. This box I'm holding contains all of the items I'll use for your examination. Before each step, I'll explain what the procedure is and you can tell me if you want to go through with it or not. Do you still want to continue?"

"Yes, ma'am."

Patty withdrew a large paper drop cloth, from the box, and placed it on the floor in front of the thirteen-year-old boy.

"Please stand on this paper and remove your clothing, but keep it on the paper. This is so we can check your clothes for anything that is out of the ordinary, like twigs or hair or even blood. You can put this on after. I'll be right back." The nurse lay the green gown on the end of the exam table.

With heavy legs, Rex managed to take the three steps from the door to the drop cloth on the floor. His hands trembled as he pulled his shirt up over his chest. The shirt caught on his chin. He paused in the blackout for a moment. Inside he felt a vast emptiness, his private universe of nothing. Noise from outside the door startled him and he continued to undress making sure each article of clothing stayed on the sheet of paper.

On the counter across from him, brown paper bags were stacked neatly, for the contents to come. The nurse came back in and looked at him with kind eyes.

"Thank you for being so careful with your clothes. You can sit right here while I pick them up." She stretched latex gloves over her hands and placed each piece of clothing in a separate bag.

Rex sat on the edge of the exam table, wincing as his bottom touched the cold, hard surface.

"Rex, the first thing I'm going to do is scan your body to see if there are traces of anything that could be of importance. I'm just going to go over your skin and in your hair. Is that OK?"

"Yes."

The nurse surveyed every inch of Rex's medium frame searching for anything that seemed unusual. Dirt, twigs, hair, scratches, clothing fibers. He watched trance-like while she delicately lifted his hand and scraped under each fingernail and placed the tiny particles into a zip-lock bag.

"For the next step, I'll swab the inside of your mouth. This one goes between your lip and bottom teeth." She held up a long skinny stick with cotton on the end of it. "This is where we check for other people's saliva." Rex started to rub his tongue in the area she just mentioned but stopped himself, thinking it might wash away something important.

She held up a second swab. "With this one, I'll collect your saliva by rubbing it across the inside of your cheek. Is it all right for me to go ahead and do these two swabs?"

"Yes."

"Rex, you're doing great. I know this isn't pleasant, but we're almost finished. I need you to go ahead and lay back now." Rex lay back and stared out at nothing in particular, his blurry vision obscured the room and made it dream-like, which he welcomed.

"OK, Rex, we are at the most invasive part now, it's very important. I need to check and swab around your penis and your rectum. It might be painful given what has happened. I promise it won't take long. Do you want to do this part?" Rex nodded. A tear escaped and rolled down his temple into his matted hair.

The nurse pushed his hospital gown to the side exposing Rex's genitals.

"Rex, you're doing great. Now bring your knees up to your chest. Can you do that for me? It's almost over."

Rex pulled his knees up and held onto his shins. His stomach tightened, and finally, his eyes closed as she administered the procedure. In the darkness he felt like he was tumbling down a long corridor bouncing from side to side, unable to stop himself. He frantically tried to grasp onto something, anything that would catch him. The nurse touched his hand and he stopped.

"All done. Just rest for a minute while I finish up over here. You did great." The nurse fixed his gown and covered him with an additional blanket.

Grandpa met him at the exam room so Rex would not have to walk alone to the lobby where grandma and Roger were waiting. "Come on mama, let's get this boy home."

Weeks passed, and Rex was still not able to function in a normal day. The molestation sent him hurtling down an ever more ruinous path and embedded itself into his psyche. He stopped going to school and began making more deviant choices.

"I know you hate school. I hate school too, but we have to go." Roger threw a branch into the pond. "And, I can't do everything around the farm either, Grandpa needs your help too!"

In the best way he knew how, Roger was trying to get Rex out of his funk.

"No, we don't have to go to school, and I don't care about the farm!"

"You're going to get us both in trouble," beseeched Roger, hoping to make Rex understand what he was doing.

Rex wouldn't listen to Roger's admonishment. Instead, Rex ended up persuading his brother to join him in his criminal activity. Their law-breaking escapades of stealing and vandalism became reckless until finally, they crossed the line. A year after the molestation, the boys were arrested for breaking into a home and stealing money.

That was the last straw. Rex and his brother became too much for their grandparents to handle. With sadness and relief, grandma packed their suitcases, loaded the boys on a Greyhound bus and shipped them to California to live with their dad and his new girlfriend, Ann and her two kids, Jimmy and Lori.

5

CALIFORNIA

"You guys get set, I'll be right back, I have to piss," Rex said as he ran into the house. The shadows were long, but there was still time to play a game; Over-the-Line baseball was a frequent recreation for the boys in the neighborhood. Rushing out of the bathroom he bumped into eleven-year-old Lori. "Sorry," he said and bolted out the front door, leaving it wide open.

"Mom, those boys pee on the floor, it's gross. Why did they have to move in with us anyway?" Lori asked her mother, Ann, who walked by the bathroom as Lori was rinsing out the dirty sink. "And what's wrong with Rex's teeth? Why do they have those brown streaks in them?"

"It was just time for them to come and be with their dad," Ann answered. "His teeth are like that because there wasn't enough fluoride in the water where he used to live. That's what I was told." Ann met Lendy when he began working at the furniture store where she worked. After becoming romantically involved, Lendy moved in with her.

"Well, Jimmy shouldn't have to share his room with them, they stink!"

"Your brother will be just fine," Ann said of her 13-year-old, straight-A son. "Just think, now you won't have to clean the pool. I'll make them do it." Ann turned the corner into the living room. "Right after I teach them how to close the front door," she said to herself. "You boys be careful in the street," Ann shouted before closing the door.

"Let's go." Rex took a couple of practice swings then stepped up to the mark. He held his bat high, like a naturally gifted athlete, and waited for Jimmy to throw the dense-foamy ball. The first pitch was outside; Rex swung and fouled onto the sidewalk. "OK Jimmy, right down the pipe this time."

Jimmy combed his fingers through his thin blonde hair, "This one will be on the money."

The neighborhood boys played Over-the-Line most days after school. Rex and Roger managed to complete the year without getting into trouble, but when summer came, Roger went to work at the furniture store, and Rex reverted to old behaviors of drinking and stealing.

One summer day, Jimmy spread his Baseball cards out, in neat rows of five, across the avocado shag carpet. While Jimmy was explaining who the players were and how one player's card was more valuable than other players, Rex realized they were the only ones home."Hey, Jimmy, watch this."

"What are you doing?"

"I'm going to steal some of my dad's whiskey," Rex boasted, tossing the Dodger's card onto the carpet.

"You are?" Jimmy gathered up his baseball cards and followed Rex to the dining room.

"Yeah, I used to do it all the time." Without reservation, Rex bent down underneath the counter that separated the dining room from the kitchen, opened the door to the almost hidden cupboard and pulled out a whiskey bottle from Lendy's collection."Have you ever had some?"

"No." Jimmy leaned closer as Rex scanned the bottle and found what he thought would be the best place to draw an almost undetectable line where the liquid measured.

"Come on." Rex walked over to the sink. "Grab that pencil."

Jimmy snagged the pencil laying on the notepad near the phone and gave it to Rex, who marked the bottle, then filled a tall, blue, plastic cup, equivalent to six shots. "Wanna try it?"

"No," *That's my chocolate milk cup,* Jimmy thought, as Rex replaced what he pilfered with water, hoping his dad would not be able to tell the difference, although Rex knew better. He just didn't care.

Standing over the kitchen sink, Rex lifted the cup and hailed, "Cheers." He tilted his head back and consumed every last drop.

"Dude." Jimmy couldn't grasp what Rex had just done. Whiskey and being drunk were foreign to him.

"Woooooeeeehh!" Rex wiped the dribble from his chin.

The next day, when Rex saw his dad going to the tucked away cupboard, he nonchalantly went to his room and waited. "Let's see how long it takes my dad to come in," he said to Jimmy. Rex knew his dad would inspect the bottle.

Sure enough, Lendy found the dot revealing the container had been tampered with and immediately boiled with rage.

"Rex, I am going to kick your ass," Lendy bellowed, as he stormed down the hall.

Rex tensed up, bracing for what was to come. Lendy entered the room with his fist clenched, demanding Rex admit he had taken the whiskey.

Rex denied the charge, infuriating his dad even more. "You lying piece of shit," Lendy boomed, as he came down on Rex with full wrath; he punched, kicked, and beat Rex into submission.

It wasn't the taking from his stash, as much as it was the lying, that resulted in such harsh punishment. The beatings were severe because Rex would fight until he was subdued.

"Man, Rex," Jimmy said. "You just kept fighting. I can't believe you didn't run and hide." Rex grinned at wide-eyed Jimmy and collapsed onto the bed.

While walking to the park one day, Rex confided just a little bit to Jimmy.
"I hate my dad." Rex tossed the football up. "I wish he was dead," Rex said, in as tough a manner as he could.

"I never knew someone who got beat up by their dad," Jimmy said with deep concern. The violence began after Rex stole the whiskey. Before that, Lendy wasn't mean. It was Rex who brought out this different side to Lendy. Jimmy scuffled with that truth. But, he was sure, a dad should not treat their child so terribly.

"My dad's an idiot and I hate him." Rex was used to his dad's abuse. Not knowing what to say, Jimmy just listened.

Rex kicked off his sandals and left them at the edge of the parking lot, the dewy grass felt soft on his feet. "Go out for a pass." He spread his fingers between the laces and threw a perfect spiral to Jimmy in the middle of the park, careful not to interfere with the rainbow-colored kites that were twirling in the wind.

6

COLORADO

About a year after Rex and Roger went to live at Ann's house with their dad and Ann's family, in California, they all moved to Colorado. Lendy had friends in Denver and he decided it would be a good place to make a living in the furniture/auction business. They sold all of their household goods, packed the necessities, piled in the cars and drove east over the Rocky Mountains.

Ann and Lendy rented a decent house in the Hidden Lake neighborhood of Westminster, north of Denver. It was the summer of 1975. Roger, 17, Rex, 15 and Jimmy, 14, slept on the floor in the large basement. Lori, 12, had her own room upstairs, where she doubled over blankets and made a cushion to sleep on.

After school and on weekends the kids on the block would hang out in the street and talk. "Hey you guys, I got some weed. You wanna get high down at the lake tonight?" Rex asked the kids standing around. It was by the lake at the end of the lane where they would smoke cigarettes and pot and consume alcohol. Out of sight of the homes, it made for a good party spot. The teenagers agreed to meet at 7 P.M. "Cool. I'm gonna bring Lori, too, and get her stoned for the first time."

After dinner, the gang met at the Lake. It was there that Rex showed Lori how to hold the end of the joint between her thumb and index finger. "You don't hold it like a cigarette," he instructed. After each kid hit off the joint, they would hold their breath and jet off running until they fell down about to faint, a guaranteed head rush. That night, with Rex by her side, Lori too, experienced the magical place of floating away.

Along with being a party planner, Rex was also a prankster. One day after school, Lori was hanging out at her friend Mindy's house close to the end of the block. They were in Mindy's front yard when Rex came rushing around the corner.

"Rusty's been stabbed," Rex said in a low frantic voice, his friend hoisted over his shoulder.

"What?" Mindy questioned

"What happened?" Lori asked.

"We were trying out some weed, Rusty put a bud in his pocket and the dude pulled a knife," Rex answered, trying to hold his composure. "I need to get him in the house."

Aghast, they all scrambled to the house. The boys turned down the hall and into a bedroom. "Get me some alcohol, I have to clean this wound," Rex yelled out to Mindy and Lori. The girls rummaged through the bathroom and brought Rex a container of Isopropyl.

"Not that kind," Rex scoffed. "Get me some whiskey."

The girls were alarmed by the news of their friend being stabbed and not thinking clearly, they delivered some of Mindy's parents' stash, as Rex ordered. A minute later both boys came out hoisting the bottle, cracking up at the girls for being naive, and proud of themselves for pulling off their stunt.

One night when the parents were out, Rex invited some friends over to party in the basement. Everybody was drinking and smoking pot, however, Rex had also taken something else. It was in Colorado that Rex branched out to harder drugs, and became addicted to shooting up heroin and taking acid. When all the friends were gone and it was just Roger, Rex, Jimmy and Lori at home, Rex snapped. He stripped down to his underwear and ran out into the snowy night, repeating over and over that he "wanted to watch the lake go." He thought the lake was going to move. Roger would lure him back in the house and try to talk sense into him, but couldn't. Rex was convinced the lake was going to go somewhere and kept running back outside in his underwear. Lori and Jimmy mostly watched, not knowing what to do. Finally, Roger subdued him and made him put his clothes on.

Soon after that incident, the electricity was turned off. Most of the time the refrigerator was empty, although bottles with different colored labels always lined the counter. One day, while Lendy was out, Ann packed up her two kids and moved back to California.

7

NEBRASKA

A year after Ann left Colorado and moved back to California, she reunited with Lendy and moved to Tulsa, Oklahoma, where he and Rex and Roger were living, it was early 1977. Lori and her brother Jimmy stayed in California with their dad and stepfamily. In the fall of that year, the relationship between Lendy and his sons deteriorated to the point they could no longer live in the same house. Roger moved to Nebraska, where he found work with a cousin, and Rex enlisted in the Navy.

The recruiter in Tulsa informed Rex there would be drug testing and even the slightest detection of illegal substances would ruin his military career. That knowledge combined with the determination to get away from his dad, motivated him to sober up. He had denied his habit for two weeks before, so he could do it again. When he knew his system was clean, he officially joined the Navy. Upon reporting to bootcamp at the Recruit Training Command, in Great Lake, Illinois, he had no worries about taking the drug test during P-days and passed all his medical exams with above-average scores. He processed in feeling fit and healthy.

It was a big change to the unstructured lifestyle he was used to, but he worked hard, kept his head down and followed orders. Rex much preferred the tech classes, where he learned water survival and weapons training, over the academic classroom study that bored him. He could bounce a quarter off of his bedsheets. His uniforms were pressed with perfect creases, and his shoes were the shiniest in his berthing compartment.

The demands of bootcamp and the hours of marching and physical activity kept his mind occupied and alleviated his drug cravings. He felt better than he had in a long time. He flourished in the highly organized environment. A natural leader, he gained respect from his fellow recruits and praise from his Recruit Division Commanders. He was on his way to a promising career.

He was proud when his name was called during the Pass in Review ceremony, although only his fellow recruits heard it. No one from his family came to celebrate his entrance into the United States Navy. He felt a fleeting twinge of sadness but knew he was better off not having the negative influences of drugs and alcohol that his family would bring. While his fellow sailors went on Liberty with their families after graduation, he chose to go straight to his next assignment. He read through his follow-on orders one more time and packed his belongings. He would be departing for his next phase of training the following day.

Rex and a fellow enlistee boarded the bus in the early morning. They became friends during Hell Week, when they encouraged each other and studied together. Neither knew the other was a drug addict until that bus ride, where they confided in each other throughout the long trip.

That simple conversation was all it took to reawaken the monster within them. The two young men decided they deserved a good high, a graduation present to themselves. When they arrived at their hotel in New York where they were to spend the night, before continuing on the next morning, they succumbed to their drug urge. The cunning, baffling and powerful compulsion hurled them to a seedy part of town to score heroin. It lured them to a dumpster behind a veterinary clinic in search of a needle. "Shit, this was probably used for a horse -— it'll work." Rex wiped the large needle on his T-shirt. " Give me the H."

The young men didn't make it back in time to catch the bus taking them to their base. When they finally did return to the hotel two days later, their belongings were in storage. Because the boys showed up late to their assigned base, they were reprimanded and put on probation. Rex continued to shoot up heroin, which caused him to flunk his trial period. He was kicked out of the Navy only months after his enlistment.

Flunking out of the military, Rex moved to Nebraska, to work driving a grain truck, joining Roger and his cousin. Roger secured his brother work at a milling corporation and they were making ends meet in the tiny apartment they shared. Content in their simple life. Then everything changed.

One day, the boss at the alfalfa company told his crew he was shutting down early due to the weather and they could go home. Rex hung the keys to the grain truck on a pegboard in the dispatch office, stomped the dust off his boots, and started thinking about what kind of alcohol he was thirsty for on this rainy Monday. Would he order a Jack and Coke, a beer or a straight-up shot of tequila? He hopped in his truck and on the way to the bar sang at the top of his lungs to the songs on the radio. The reception was terrible and created a lot of static, but he didn't care. He slapped the steering wheel with his fingertips keeping time with the beat and occasionally added a double-time or a syncopation that would make him late to start back on the one beat. He loved music, especially quirky off mainstream bands and southern rock.

He pulled in to the parking space on the gravel lot where he usually parked, eager to start partying. Because it was earlier than usual, most of "the regulars" he hung out with weren't there yet. It was a small dimly lit tavern with a couple of pool tables, one dartboard, a jukebox, and no windows. He punched up a new Bob Dylan song.

"There's a long-distance train rolling through the rain," Rex sang along as he sat down at the bar and ordered a beer.

"Some storm brewing out there," said the bartender engaging in small talk.

"Yeah, fine with me though, made us have to quit early."

"Well, we can always use the rain, said the bartender, who was rinsing three mugs at a time in a basin of water. "Ready for another one?"

Rex conversed with the bartender but kept his eye on the door as the dingy pub became occupied with familiar faces. At 4:00, in walked the person he was waiting for: the dope man. Rex waved him over.

"I want to score some blotter," Rex said leaning in close.

"You've come to the right person, got a full supply."

"Well, then, let's take a walk outside."

"I'm following you."

"Watch my beer for me, will you?" Rex asked the bartender. "I'll be right back." He went outside with his dealer.

He bought a hit of LSD and placed it under his tongue until it dissolved into his system. This particular brand was a "creeper" and without being conscious of it, the drug eased Rex into the alternate state he loved, the magical place of floating away. His senses became heightened and his surroundings became a vivid palette of sounds and colors. It was a parallel universe; he wished he could live there always. Without a care in the world and feeling light on his feet, Rex drank more beer, shot a few games of pool, and carried on with the other lushes who came for their nightly escape. After the 2 a.m. last call, Rex stayed and smoked one more joint in the parking lot with a small group of hardcore drug addicts like himself. He arrived home barely coherent and stumbled into bed a couple of hours before daybreak.

It was Tuesday, October 3, 1978. He had been asleep for just a short time when the phone rang: his boss saying he needed Rex to come to work. The weather cleared earlier than expected, and his boss wanted to get a jump on the day to make up for lost production. It was a good job and Rex didn't want to jeopardize his employment. Instead of telling his boss he could use some more shut-eye, he dragged himself out of bed, took a cold shower, and reported in for work. When he arrived at the silo, his truck was being filled with grain. Rex was to haul it across town to the distribution yard.

Twenty minutes down the lonely interstate, Rex passed out cold from the hard night of partying and lack of sleep. His truck veered off the lane, flipped over, landed back on the asphalt and skidded for a hundred feet. The sound of metal screeching along the pavement jolted him awake, and he could see a blanket of sparks spreading across the blacktop until the out-of-control rig slammed into a cement embankment at the end of a one-lane bridge. The impact of the crash ruptured the gas tank and caved in the large cab, trapping Rex underneath.

He was drenched in eighty-five gallons of gas, his legs pinned under the dashboard. He could not feel them, nor free himself from the twisted metal.

Rex could not fight off the looming thoughts of death and succumbed to the very real possibility that he would die on that deserted stretch of highway, scared, alone, and soaked in gasoline. As pitiful as his life was, it was all he had and he wanted to keep it.

He thought it was forever, but after fifteen minutes a gentleman on his way to work drove by, saw the wreck and hurried for help. Two small fire trucks and an ambulance arrived on the scene. The rescue team worked the whole morning to cut Rex out of the truck with the Jaws of Life. The cab was very unstable. The crew calculated each cut and demolition precisely to keep the truck from caving in on Rex or ignite the dripping fuel.

While he was alert he could hear the shrilling sound of the chain saw as workers labored to extricate him from the vehicle. In between cuts, he could hear talking in the distance, but couldn't make out what they were saying. One of the first responders moved close to him and let him know that they were working as fast as they could, and to hang in there. The medic also told Rex that his brother and his boss had arrived on the scene. That was comforting to Rex, but he was scared that he would not make it out of the buckled cab alive.

Out of the corner of his eye, Rex could see Roger staring at the scene before him in disbelief, distraught and unable to speak, as the rescue workers stood on top of the truck, cut up the cab and carefully remove crumpled sections of Rex's rig.

Rex was taken to a small rural hospital where it was assessed that his left leg had been crushed above the knee. To save his leg, a metal rod was inserted to hold it in place. Too swollen and mangled, the large gash that spanned the length of his outer thigh could not be stitched together and a piece of pigskin lay unsecured over the exposed mutilated tissue to keep it protected from infection.

Within hours of getting the phone call that no parent wants to receive, Lendy and Ann were packed and in the car, hurrying to Rex.

The third night they were there, Roger started messing around with the blood pressure device hanging on the wall behind Rex's bed. He pulled the rubber tube out of the clear plastic apparatus, sucked in the deepest breath he could, and he blew into the eight-inch long hose. He ran the red ball up the cylinder almost to the top. It was a welcome lighthearted moment. When Roger finished, he handed the device to Rex for his turn.

Ann, Lendy, and Roger watched and cheered as Rex sucked in until his chest was tight and his face was red. He blew into the tube as hard as he could, pushing until every bit of air was drained from his lungs. The red ball went halfway to the top.

The internal pressure caused the whole side of his injured leg to explode and start hemorrhaging. The laughter turned to panic as buzzers sounded and nurses ran in to see what happened. The pigskin that lay over the gaping wound was not enough to keep gangrene from riddling his leg. Blood and puss were streaming out of his thigh, gushing down the bed and pouring on to the floor.

"Code blue, code blue," one nurse yelled. Another unlocked the brakes on the bed wheels and spun it in a half-circle to line up straight with the door. In disbelief, Ann, Lendy, and Roger watched horror-stricken as the nurses hurried to push the bed to the operating room for emergency surgery, their feet trampling through the acrid body fluid.

For hours the family braced themselves for the worst: he would not live through the night. The clinic was ill-equipped to handle such extreme trauma and Rex was merely replenished with enough blood to keep him alive. The staff simply did not know what else to do. Ann, Lendy, and Roger were relieved Rex had not died but knew it was imperative he be moved to a bigger hospital.

When he was stable, Ann and Lendy hired an air ambulance to fly him from Nebraska to a trauma center in Tulsa. Roger flew with Rex in the aircraft, while Lendy and Ann drove back. When the plane arrived, the boys were met by a team of medical personnel and transported a short distance to the trauma unit.

The next day when Rex was settled in his room and sedated, Ann arrived at the hospital. She noticed his foot, black and muddled and swollen; how his toenails fringed out like bristles on a broom. She was worried about Rex seeing his foot like that and pulled the sheet over it. Each time she covered his foot he would pull the sheet off to examine it, trying to reconcile that what he saw was real and not something he was imagining. He knew what his foot was supposed to look like and that wasn't it.

While Ann was there keeping him company, Rex's mother, Pauline, came into the room. Knowing that Rex needed his mother at a time like this, Ann was happy she came.

Rex's mother held his hand and with her other hand stroked his hair. She softly asked, "How are you?"

Barely opening his eyes, he peeked at each of the women and uttered, "This is the most beautiful moment of my life. Both my moms are here."

That was the only time his mother came to care for him. After that, she sent a preacher to pray with him in the afternoons. When Ann inquired why he was there, the preacher told her, "Rex's mom asked him to come and pray with Rex." Rex couldn't comprehend why his mom wasn't coming and didn't like that she sent a preacher in her place.

One day when the minister came, Rex looked at Ann and protested, "I don't want this stranger in here saying prayers. I don't know why he is coming." He asked Ann to tell him to stop.

"We appreciate you coming, but we're concerned why Rex's mom isn't coming herself," Ann told the preacher.

"She told me that she isn't allowed to come here," the preacher said defensively.

"No, that's not true. We would love for her to come here."

"Someone told her, she couldn't come," the annoyed preacher reiterated.

"Well, I don't know anything about that. I appreciate what you are trying to do for Rex and being supportive of his mother, but don't come back! You're upsetting Rex," Ann firmly said.

"Nobody's ever talked to me like that," huffed the minister as he turned and left the room."

"Thank you," said Rex, as he and Ann smiled at each other and chuckled.

Even though the infection spread to his thigh, the doctors desperately wanted to save his knee. After much consultation with Rex and his family, they decided to amputate just below the patella. A BK amputation would allow him to still have the use of his knee joint. A few days after the surgery it was evident that the gangrene was not diminishing and his knee could not be saved. He was operated on again and the surgeon amputated above the knee, confident all the gangrene had been eradicated. It wasn't. The third time his leg was cut just below the hip, leaving him with only a short stump. In extreme pain and distraught that his whole left leg had just been cut off, and he was now a cripple, there was one thing he could count on – the reality-numbing morphine drip.

8

TULSA

When Rex, 18, came home from the hospital in late 1978, Roger had moved from Nebraska to Tulsa and was living with Ann and Lendy. Rex and Roger's older sister Lisa, was also living with Lendy and Ann in Tulsa. She was engaged to be married. Lori 15, had also moved to Tulsa. It didn't take long for Lori to see that Rex was down and out, struggling. Remembering how athletic and agile he was when they all lived in California, she felt bad for him and became Rex's assistant. Lori pushed his wheelchair, brought him his food, picked up after him, fetched his cigarettes, and told him to shower when he stank. Because

Rex hated to wear his ill-fitted and heavy full-leg prosthetic, Lori would make sure his crutches were always within arm's length. He didn't have to lift a finger, even though he could get around on his crutches just fine and easily drive his truck when they went somewhere.

Lori was right there to do everything for him; in an unhealthy way, it gave her a sense of purpose. She didn't know she was becoming codependent to Rex and enabling him in a lazy, entitled lifestyle. There were times, though, he annoyed her and she would leave him to fend for himself.

One cold, blustery day Rex and Lori wanted to get loaded. Their parents were home so they couldn't risk going into the garage and taking hits off the bong like they normally did. Instead, they bundled up in their beanies and jackets and braved the winter snowstorm. "We're going outside," Lori yelled, then hurried out the door before someone asked why. Her hands throbbed from the frigid air like they were being smashed with a hammer, making it painful to grip the wheelchair handles and push Rex through the two-inch slushy ridges of brown snow built up on the road from tire tracks, and for the first time, the end of the block seemed a long way away. The thought of being high kept them motivated until they reached their destination.

Rex pinched the end of the joint with his index finger and thumb, like he had shown Lori back in Colorado, leaving just enough sticking out, to inhale from. He breathed in slow and steady until his lungs were filled then topped the toke off with one last quick inhale. His chest still tight from holding the smoke, he gestured the joint toward Lori, "Here ya go, man." She took the joint and did the same thing. Three hits each and it was gone.

Sufficiently stoned, Lori turned Rex and his wheelchair around to go home, but when she started pushing, the wheels wouldn't turn. "Come on, shit," griped Rex.

"I'm trying. It's snowing," Lori backed up her feet and straightened out her arms, her stance more like she was going to dive into a swimming pool, than push a wheelchair. That gave her more body leverage to propel the wheelchair over the initial hump and get rolling.

"Try har..., watch where you're going. Damn it." A rock abruptly stopped the wheelchair, causing Rex to jolt forward and almost fall out of the seat.

After a couple of hard lurches, Lori built some momentum and they were on their way. She laughed over the bumpy start. Rex was irritated.

"It's not funny. What's wrong with you?"

"Me! See ya, asshole."

Annoyed by his buzz-kill, bossy attitude, Lori left him out in the middle of the street to toil through the guck himself. She went inside situated herself on the couch, in the warm living room, and peered at him through the big picture window, snickering as she saw him struggle.

"What are you laughing at?" Lisa walked into the front room carrying a travel bag, her thin red hair pinned back at the sides.

"Rex out in the street. He can't get going. He was being an idiot, so I left him out there."

"That should teach him to be nicer. I'm going to Pete's. I'm going to stay the night over there."

"Have fun." Lori turned her attention back to Rex.

Rex's icy breath solidified into a fog that swirled around his head as he panted trying to get his chair rolling. He leaned forward and clasped his hands way back on the wheel, so he would have a longer push stroke, thinking that would help get him started. It didn't. Then he placed his palms on the top of the wheels, the cold metal stinging his skin, and used a faster rolling motion, that got him going until he banged into another rock and halted abruptly. Rex, red with anger, glared at Lori, as she grinned and waved. When he finally made it inside the house, he went straight to Lori.

"What the fuck was that, leaving me out there in the street?" Rex whispered so the folks wouldn't hear him.

"That's what you get for being an a-hole." Lori handed him his crutches.

The two smoked pot and drank together regularly. Rex did not do hard drugs in front of Lori nor did she observe him swallow pills, although she knew about the prescription painkillers. When they went out, it was usually with her sidekicks. He never took Lori to the dope dealer's house or to the homes of people he hung out with.

Despite all the dysfunction, Lori's mom, Ann, maintained that she never fretted about Lori when she was with Rex. Intuitively, Ann knew he would not let anything happen to her daughter and he didn't. If not the best of influence Rex was a protector. Ann saw that trait in him.

Rex had been home from the hospital for about eight months, when, in June of 1979, Lori completed her sophomore year at Tulsa East Side High School. She then went back to visit her family in California for the summer, where she decided to stay and finish her junior and senior years of high school, living with her dad and stepfamily.

In the fall of 1980, when Jimmy, Lori's brother, was 19 and already graduated from high school, he moved from

California to Tulsa to find a job and start his life as an adult. Contrary to Lori, he witnessed Rex, now 20, ingest every kind of pill imaginable, whether he knew what they were or not. For months, Jimmy and Rex spent every day getting loaded and "hustling." They would meander through neighborhoods in Rex's truck hunting for appliances and furniture in garages and yards. When they ran across something interesting, they would stop and inquire about the item. More times than not, the homeowner was glad to dispense of the piece of junk taking up space.

They would buy the items for cheap, fix them up, and sell them for a profit. The garage, looking more like a second-hand store, than a place to park cars, was filled with refrigerators, stoves, dishwashers and an assortment of antiques the previous owners had no idea the value of.

Rex and Jimmy would spend hours repairing, scrubbing and restoring old relics into tip-top shape for resale. They both developed entrepreneurial skills and it was a good business for a time, until the drinking and getting high became the most important activity of the day. The unhealthy lifestyle was taking its toll on Jimmy,

"What are you doing?" Rex surprised to see Jimmy packing.

"Leaving, man. Going back to California." Jimmy zipped up the suitcase.

"Why, what happened?"

"Nothing happened, that's the problem. I don't want to sit around and get high all day." Jimmy picked up his suitcase and went to the front door. "I came here to get away from that shit."

"Dude, you're leaving, just like that? You haven't even been here that long." Rex followed Jimmy to his car.

"I've been here eight months and three days and it's not working out."

"What about your mom?"

"When she gets home, tell her I'll call when I get back to California. Take care of yourself man." Rex, confused and heavy-hearted, stood leaning on his crutches and watched Jimmy drive away. It was April 1981.

Lori graduated high school in California, June 1981, and moved back to Tulsa that same summer before going into the Air Force. During the two years that Lori was living in California, Rex gained mobility, independence and began to challenge himself physically. The family often spent time at Keystone Lake where they would fish and water ski. One hot August day, family, and friends, Kathi, Jim and Richie, loaded up the old weather-worn Bay Liner with snacks, beer, fishing gear, and water skis. They hitched the boat to the truck and embarked on a full day at the lake.

After spending the first few hours sitting in the boat fishing but not catching any, it was finally time to ski. Lendy drove the boat around the lake until he found a large cove, where the water was smooth as glass and reflected like a mirror. No other boats were in sight. You could go straight for a long way before having to turn around. The perfect place to ski was all theirs. Lori went first. Suited up, she jumped in the water, positioned herself, and up and out of the water she came. She slalomed cutting back and forth across the wake each time creating a large spray behind her, enjoying a long and satisfying ride.

Then, one by one, the others went, leaving Rex for last. Stubborn, there was no way he was going to watch the others and not go himself. He buckled up the yellow life vest, plopped into the lake and inserted his one foot into the back boot of the slalom ski. Lori threw him the single handle rope. Lendy lined up the boat and waited for him to say, "hit it." The others looked on in anticipation and were not surprised when the rope was yanked out of his hands and he fell over sideways. Ann raised the flag, Lendy pushed the throttle forward and quickly circled back. Lori reached over the side of the boat and grabbed the rope.

"That's all right, make sure you lean way back and pull your knee in close to your chest," Lori instructed as she flung the rope handle to Rex.

Rex yelled "Hit it," and again the rope went flying, like a snake wriggling in the air, and he tumbled over butt side up. Lendy looped around and Lori tossed Rex the line.

"That was better. Don't try to stand up too fast, let the boat pull you," encouraged Lori.

"Come on Rex, you can do it," cheered Kathi.

"OK," yelled Rex, who pitched forward this time. "Fuck'n shit." Frustrated, he smacked the water with his hand. "Give me that rope."

"Go." Rex toppled head first again. "I'm done. Take the stupid ski."

"Oh, man you're so close." Lori gathered up the rope.

"You're not getting in the boat until you stand up," snapped Lendy. Rex hadn't seen that look in a long time.

"Toss me the damn rope."

A determined Rex pulled his knee to his chest, leaned back, pinched his elbows in tight, pursed his lips and nodded. Lendy pushed the lever all the way forward, the engine revved, the bow pointed to the sky, then leveled out when the boat picked up speed. With fingers crossed everyone in the boat watched, riveted, to see if Rex would stand up and ski. Then, at the same time, they all thrust their arms high up in the air.

"Woo hoo." Jim pumped his fists in the air.

71

"Way to go, Rex, shouted Kathi." Rex could see their overjoyed faces witnessing him glide across the water.

"I knew you could do it, whooped Richie." The long, shimmering, golden line of the sun's reflection on the water trailed behind Rex's wake.

Rex hunched over giving some relief to his tired back, squishing his gut, now big from months of inactivity. His bright red swim trunks were longer than his stump and flopped in the wind where there normally would be a leg. He looked off-balance – lopsided. Rex straightened up and pulled his elbows back and for a little while longer basked in the glorious moment of victory. When he was finished, he hurled the rope handle and collapsed from exhaustion. Lori pulled him into the boat, Kathi tossed him a towel and cracked him a beer. It was a good day.

For the few minutes Rex was skiing, he felt normal again. Gliding across the water made him forget, for the first time, that he was missing a leg. Even if only for a brief time, skiing that day gave him hope, that just maybe he was going to be OK

9

TULSA PART TWO

The long clammy summer gave way to the first leaves dropping from the Oak trees. It was September 9, 1981, Rex was melancholy about Lori leaving for the Air Force. There were a couple of hours until she needed to leave for the bus station.

Rex took her for one last ride in his yellow Ford pickup. It was out of alignment and pulled hard to the right making it difficult to guide. "When I drove your truck, I had to hold the steering wheel tight," said Lori.

"Yeah, I gotta get that fixed." Rex knew she was just making small talk rather than sit in the discomfort of the moment. He followed her lead.

"Remember that time a couple of years ago when we got stuck four-wheeling?" asked Rex.

"How could I forget, I totally had a crush on Richie. I was nervous sitting so close to him."

"What, you never said anything."

"I was embarrassed. Then I had to stay with him while you went and called the tow truck. That was a crazy night."

"Speaking of boys, you know there are some real jerks?" Rex said.

"Yeah, I know."

"Good, just be careful who you hang around with."

"I will."

"You're gonna have a long bus ride. Let's get you something to pass the time," Rex said, changing the subject.

"Sounds good to me," Lori smiled.

After their trip down memory lane, they stopped at a liquor store where Rex bought her a pint of Jack Daniel's green label, her going-away present. She thought it was the coolest thing a big brother could do.

"Hide that in your purse, I don't want your mom to find out."

They arrived back to the house with just enough time for Lori to put her bags in the car, her "gift" hidden in her purse. Rex leaned on his crutches and this time watched Lori leave.

***

Now that Lori was gone, Rex was the lone kid at home. A year had passed since Jimmy moved back to California, Roger had also left Tulsa and his older sister, Lisa, was married and raising two toddlers. Rex felt lonely and trapped in the thick, lifeless haze of addiction, his soul starved of the nourishment of connection. There was one activity that could penetrate his armor of darkness – spending time with his young niece and nephew.

He visited his sister and niece and nephew regularly and thought Lisa to be the most stable one in the family. Her conventional life was a welcome reprieve from his own disarrayed situation. He trusted her and therefore asked her to hold on to the settlement money he received from his accident. She could then monitor to make sure it was spent properly. If he blew all of his monthly disability check on drugs or other unnecessary whims, he was cut off until his next allotment.

75

It pained Lisa to see her brother's downward spiral after his accident. She wanted to help him and knew that her children loved their uncle, so she let him come over whenever he wanted, but kept a watchful eye, knowing he would most likely be loaded.

In the spring of 1982, his niece and nephew, four and five-years-old, were still innocent and untarnished by the woes the world can bring. He cherished being around them and seeing them experience joy in the simplest of ways – observing a grasshopper jump across the porch, eating an ice cream cone before it melted down their hands. It got him out of the house, where he hated living with his dad and Ann, and released him temporarily from his ugly existence and reminded him that life could still be gratifying.

Rex would sit on the floor and horse around with them until every toy they owned was pulled out of the toy chest and scattered across the carpet.

One day, skin-crawling and desperate for a hit of anything, Rex fabricated a story to get money for drugs. He called his sister, panic in his voice. "I have to come over and get some money."

"For what, Rex? What's wrong?" asked Lisa. She held the phone receiver between her shoulder and ear while spreading jelly on a slice of white bread.

"I owe the dealer." Rex braced himself for his sister's response.

"You know I am not going to give you money for that." Lisa gave her kids each a peanut butter and jelly sandwich.

"You don't understand, he said he'd kill me if I don't pay him by tonight."

"What? Rex don't you dare come over here, someone might be following you." Lisa set two cups of milk on the kitchen table, one for each of her children.

"What am I supposed to do?"

"Call the police. But, don't you come over here, I mean it. And Rex, as much as it hurts me to say this, I will no longer look the other way. You can't see the kids anymore, not until you get yourself together."

She didn't know if he was making that up, regardless she lost all trust in him and certainly the people he hung around with. As a mother, she was not willing to risk harm to her children.

Rex couldn't register what he was hearing. He felt like he'd been sucker-punched in the stomach. When his sister told him he could not come over and spend time with his niece and nephew unless he stopped using drugs, he had a moment of confusion. What did she mean he couldn't see his niece and nephew if he was high? Didn't she know he was more stable when he was primed? That it would be worse for the kids if he came over on a day when he hadn't evened out his mental state with a little bit of heroin, or meth, or whatever kind of pills were in his pocket?

Rex's denial was pegging at full capacity. "What? I have a legal right as an uncle to see my niece and nephew." He pleaded his case and tried to manipulate her from every angle he could think of.

"No, you don't." Lisa gave her kids a cherry popsicle. She almost blurted a laugh at how ridiculous her brother's statement was.

"You can't keep your kids from being a part of their extended family."

"I'm their mother, I can do what I want." Lisa lowered her voice so her children wouldn't hear her.

Exasperated, Rex spouted out one last effort to win his argument. "No, you can't!"

"Rex, listen to yourself, you're not making any sense," scolded Lisa.

In spite of his below-the-belt tactics, she held firm to her decision. Defeated and furious, he fetched a gram of heroin from his room and went on a bender. He dealt with the all too well-known rejection in his usual manner – floating away.

When Rex came off his three-day binge and could think somewhat coherently, the toll of what his addiction was doing to him, socked in like a thick winter fog and the weight of it shattered him. It penetrated his shield of denial and forced him to look hard at who he had become; a creature who even his sister cast out. It also enabled the light of his authentic self to spill through, revealing that behind his tough-guy façade and drug-induced survival coma there beat a tender heart. For the first time in a long time, he aspired to be different. He wanted to stop escaping. With absolutely nothing to live for and a life that appeared hopelessly irredeemable, there was simply one thing left for him to do – change.

10

KEEP COMING BACK

Rex picked up the kitchen phone and stretched its long tangled cord to the dining room table. From where he sat, he could see out the large living room window into the front yard. The last signs of winter melting, as finches fluttered between the sprawling branches of budding elms, causing tiny pellets of dew to drift about. He lay his head, throbbing from a hangover, on the table, thoughts about what he would say to Lisa regarding their conversation three days ago oscillated like the birds he was watching. *What will she say? What should I say? She's going to chew my ass. Fuck, I hate this.*

Knowing he needed to resolve the situation with his sister, he lifted the phone receiver and brought it to his ear, the buzzing tone caused him to wince. He hung up before dialing and went back to watching the finches. One of his feathered friends settled on the window ledge and looked like it was admiring itself in the reflection of the glass. Rex lamented his disgust over his own reflection as he noted the pretty contrast of the bird's black and white striped wings against its rosy breast feathers.

It had been 4 years since the accident that amputated his leg. Since then he spent his time depressed or strung out with no real effort to process what happened. Now, when he inadvertently saw his reflection, he didn't recognize himself. His once angular jaw was soft and undefined, his waist hidden underneath a rotund belly. When he dared look lower, he could only see what was not there. His lean athletic form and the potential of it forever gone.

The bird flew off past the trees and landed on the telephone pole across the street. "Fuck it. I've got nothing left to lose." Rex made the call.

"Rex, you're always high on something. You disappear for days, no one knows where you are, if you're alive or dead. You can't be trusted at all. Rex, your family worries about you.

You're ruining your life and hurting the people around you." Lisa did not mince her words.

"I know. I don't mean to." His heart slashed by his older sister's truth.

"I don't know what kind of trouble you're in this time, but I'm not giving you the money." Lisa's intensity increased causing a lump to well in Rex's throat.

"OK." Rex could barely speak.

"I won't consent to my kids being put in harm's way. You hang around with bad people. If any of your friends ever show up here I will call the police," Lisa continued castigating.

"I understand. I don't want that either," Rex said sheepishly.

"You are confusing the kids, too. You say they're the best thing in your life, but then you don't show up when you say you're coming over. Or you come over and you're OK and want to play with them, then the next time you're so high all you do is sit on the couch and ignore them. I don't know what to say when they ask me if something is wrong with you. I won't let them grow up thinking this is normal behavior. I want my children to know their uncle, but not like this, not as a drug addict." Her gut-wrenching stipulation of no contact with her kids was serious.

"I don't want them to know me like this either. I'm sorry." Globes of sorrow rolled down his cheeks.

"Rex you need to go to rehab and get some help. You should go today. I'll even drive you there."

Reduced to nothing, Rex agreed. "OK. I'll find somewhere to go."

Before he changed his mind, Rex retrieved the yellow pages, tracked down a hospital that listed a detox department for drug addicts and made arrangements to check in later that day. Then, he trudged to his bedroom, packed a small bag with a few changes of clothes and some toiletries and waited for Lisa to pick him up.

In the lingering silence of the car ride, Rex wiped his finger across the dashboard making a line in the dust that had accumulated. "You're doing the right thing," counseled Lisa interrupting the awkwardness.

Rex rubbed his dirty finger on his pant leg, "If you say so." He wondered if he was and whether he was ready to stop using drugs. Now that reality was daring him, he wasn't sure. He didn't know life any other way.

Rex's uneasiness worsened as the conversation with Lisa replayed in his head. "You're confusing them... I don't want them to know you like this... what do I tell them... you need help." He opened his mouth to scream. No sound came out. At that moment it registered: he was more crippled emotionally than he was physically.

At the hospital, Lisa parked in a visitor's slot a short distance from the front entrance. People were prancing about the grounds looking purposeful, like they were ready to check off the next item on their daily "To Do" List. If Rex made a list, this certainly would not have been on it. It wasn't until they reached the front entrance and saw the post above the glass double doors that they figured out they were at a psychiatric hospital. Rex wanted to turn and run. Having just a mere drug problem, he was taken aback and didn't think he belonged with crazy people, or did he?

Past behavior flashed through his mind. The periods when he'd gotten himself so doped up that all he could do was stare at nothing for hours, oblivious to what was going on around him. He recalled the times he would try to maintain a conversation but could at best only mumble incoherently. He called to mind the stints when he did not sleep for days because he had shot up so much speed, causing him to see things that weren't there. Once while staying in a trailer out in the country, his hallucinations and paranoia were so acute that he loaded bullets into a rifle, crawled around the yard naked, and shot at people who were in his imagination. He was the same as the so-called crazy people in the psych ward.

Rex and Lisa located the elevators standing open, awaiting their arrival. They stepped in and pushed Number 3. The doors closed and up they whirred in that constricted elevator hush. The compartment stopped with a clunk and the doors opened. On the opposite wall, a sign, with an arrow pointing to the right, read Detox Center.

The long stark corridor, void of anything fruitful, matched Rex's barren soul. A repugnant concoction of vomit, urine, and disinfectant bombarded the air and burned his nostrils. As they walked through the tunnel of stench, Rex crinkled his nose. "It's going to be all right." Lisa reiterated, trying to take the strain out of the moment. *Of course she would say that; she wasn't the one staying.* Rex had his doubts.

They checked in with the admissions clerk and filled out the stack of papers clamped to a well-used clipboard with a pen tied to the top by a piece of yarn. "All done?" The clerk raised an eyebrow over the rim of his glasses.

"Yes, sir." Rex and Lisa answered at the same time.

The clerk thumbed through the application, "Looks like it's all here. Need any special accommodations?" The clerk nodded towards Rex's missing left leg.

"No."

Lisa sighed in relief, "Well, that's it." She gave Rex a good luck hug and headed back down the tunnel of stench.

Rex sat in the waiting room for a little while longer, trying not to let his mind wander to horrific conclusions about what this experience would be like. *Time, People and Readers Digest* littered the tabletops, but not much of a reader, he distracted himself from having an emotional meltdown by silently singing "Hound Dog" by Elvis Presley, just the chorus, over and over. Finally, the door labeled Patients Only opened and a nurse stepped out.

"Rex Patrick."

"Th-th-that's me."

The nurse hurried him to the blood pressure station and told him to have a seat. She wrapped the cuff snugly around his right arm. "Your blood pressure is a little high, are you nervous?" The nurse popped her chewing gum.

"You think? Hell yes, I'm nervous." The air hissed as it released from the blood pressure wrap. The nurse charted - BP 143/94, weight 247.

"Let's get you to your room."

A chair, a single bed, and a small two-drawer dresser with veneer chipped off was an upgrade from the flea-infested couch he regularly slept on at his drug buddies. The nurse inspected all of the items in his duffle bag searching for contraband. Heat stung Rex's cheeks as she scrutinized every seam of his underwear. "You're clean," she pointed at the cupboard, "You can put your things in there. The doctor will be in shortly." Clapping her hands together one time as if to say, 'job well done' she was off to another task.

Rex sat on the edge of the bed frozen in a straitjacket of fear. He had an impulse to hightail it but couldn't move. He sat there, mute, for what seemed an eternity until the doctor finally came in. His lack of bed-side manner cut through any pleasantries.

"Rex, you're going to get sick, very sick," the doctor declared in a straightforward, clinical manner, "and I am not going to do anything to stop it. On the contrary, I implore you to get so sick that you never forget what it was like." The doctor's high-pitched nasal tone clogged, even more, the already stuffy air.

"What do you mean doctor?" Rex squirmed, thinking that was an odd statement for a doctor to make.

"Rex, do you know what dope sick is?"

"Yeah. It"s like having the flu."

"It's nothing like that, Rex. Nothing." The doctor's eyes were unsympathetic.

***

Rex woke up the next day feeling the same as he usually did in the morning, foggy brained, anxious about the day, his hands slightly trembling. But, when his autopilot routine of reaching over for some pills or laying out a line didn't transpire, he was acutely reminded of the decision he had made the day before – going to rehab. In a faint whisper, Rex asked himself, "What were you thinking?" Out loud he answered, "I don't know," rolled over, and went back to sleep.

Throughout the day, clinicians checked on him, but for the most part, he was left alone. By late afternoon stomach pangs roused him up and out of his arid room, in search of food. As he ventured toward the cafeteria, mentally ill patients sitting slumped over in wheelchairs lined the halls, like a traffic jam in rush hour. It wasn't a nightmare; he really was in the psych ward. Although he didn't look out of place, a fat guy with one leg getting along on crutches, long, stringy hair shooting out every which way, he felt out of place. Knowing all too well what it was like to be confined to a wheelchair, he kept his head down and found the cafeteria.

The crusty macaroni and cheese was the only thing that looked edible, that and the iceberg lettuce labeled "salad." Not in the mood for conversation, Rex choked down his meal by himself, then went back to his room to sleep some more.

The next morning, again he felt like he usually did when he woke up, and began to wonder if the doctor was wrong about getting sick. Midway through that second day, it hit him.

Because his body had been daily contaminated from a young age with alcohol, pills, Meth, Heroin, several days would pass before he stepped out of that room again.

Four days and four nights, he tossed and turned uncontrollably in his bed. He experienced severe itching and excruciating stomach pains. At times, his body became so hot he sweat-soaked the sheets, then, as if a flip had been switched, his bones turned cold and he would shiver for hours. Losing control of his bodily functions, he vomited in a bucket and soiled the bed until all of his insides were empty. In utter despair, he screamed for someone, anyone, to come and save him. Nurses checked in on him, took his blood pressure, made sure he wasn't becoming dangerously dehydrated and changed the bedding. However, the doctor's words held true, not one of them applied measures to relieve him of his anguish.

The physical torment, as bad as it was, became overshadowed by severe psychological episodes. He grew increasingly agitated. The slightest noise of a nurse entering the room or chatter in the hall sent him into a temper tantrum. He would sling a dignity-shredding barrage of insults toward who or what committed such an atrocity. Fury boiled up in him so intensely, at times, he felt he could go into a psychotic break, ending up slumped in a wheelchair in the hall of stench. He would sob for hours for no apparent reason. His mind and body were out of control. There was nothing he could do to alleviate his agony. From time to time a nurse would say, "You have to let it run its course. You'll get through it."

By day six he started to regain his faculties. His headache subsided and he was no longer dry heaving. Rex made it through the 120-hour torrent of detoxing. He was put on a daily routine of breakfast, lunch, and dinner in the cafeteria. He attended two group therapy sessions a day and three private counseling sessions a week. He was also prompted to write in a journal, which he did.

Entry 1

I had a shit life growing up. My dad punched me, but it didn't stop me from stealing his whiskey. Sometimes I did it just to piss him off and see his face turn red. I didn't care if he was going to beat me for it. Ha, got one on you, mother fucker! One time I thought the vein in his forehead was going to pop. I was hoping it would. I wanted to see the bastard's head explode. Fuck this, I'm going to bed.

Entry 7

I wonder what Roger is doing today. I haven't talked to him for a long time, I don't even know where he is right now. We did some shit together. He was, well, I guess is, my best friend. Hmm and I don't even know where he is. I wonder if he knows where I am. Sorry, Rog, for getting us busted. It was my fault, everything is my fault…

Entry 14

About a week after I got home from the hospital, I wanted to kill myself, I had the pills in my hand ready to do it, but Ann came home. When she opened the door it startled me and I dropped half of them. I didn't tell the.....aahhh, this is bullshit!

One morning, as Rex was on his way to a therapy session, Stetson, a good-ol-boy, who chose rehab over jail, called to Rex walking down the hall. "Hey Rex, you want to meet in the community room and play some cards?"

"I can't. I'm headed to see the shrink, Dunlap. Where's your cowboy hat?"

"I was told to 'put it in my closet.' Ain't that some shit? Well, have fun spilling your guts to Dr. Funlap. Get it?" Stetson bellowed at his wordplay on the doctor's name.

"Yep." Rex, clutching his journal, continued to his appointment.

"Hey, Rex." Dr. Dunlap waved him in. "Have a seat." Rex sat down in the comfortable, worn, Naugahyde easy chair. "Oh good, you brought your diary."

"Do you have to call it that?"

"Do you have a problem with that word?"

"No, here." Rex didn't want to have a whole session on why he thought the word diary was girly.

The psychiatrist turned up his desk fan and read Rex's journal.

Entry 22

I told the group today that it was Lisa who told me to go to rehab, that she read me the riot act. I told them that she probably saved my life. Fred, the facilitator, said, "I was lucky to have a sister like her." Yeah. I still want my money, though. I wonder what the rug rats are doing right now. Oh well, goodnight.

While the doctor was reading, Rex fiddled with the Rubik's Cube from the basket of brain-benders on the doctor's desk. Turning the cube this way and that way, he spun rows around and back and forth until he got all the same colors on one side.

"Look at that, you got all the same color on one side. That's progress from last time." Doctor Dunlap handed Rex his journal. Rex put the cube back in the basket. "So, let's talk about Lisa. Do you want to talk about her? Is that why you brought your journal today?"

"Busted." Rex's smile burdened. Dr. Dunlap straightened his note pad and didn't respond. "You know, it's true, I would've never come if she hadn't made me." Rex picked the Rubik's Cube up.

"She made you?"

"She gave me an ultimatum, I never saw it coming. Fucking denial. All I had was time, I'd get so bored and lonely. I don't know what was worse, home or the drug house. At least there were people at the drug house." Rex kept spinning the squares around, checking each side to see if any more colors were lining up.

"So you were lonely?"

"Yeah, after everyone moved out and it was only me at home.

"How old are your niece and nephew?" The doctor flipped the page in his notebook.

"They're four and five. I'd go over there high as a kite. I actually believed no one would notice." Rex set the cube down and stared at the scratch lines in the brown tile floor. His body quivered.

Doctor Dunlap pushed the kleenex box to the edge of his desk. "Would you interact with the kids?"

"Yeah - I screwed most of that up, too." Rex wiped his eyes with the kleenex. That question accosted Rex with memories he didn't want to think about; the reasons why his sister revoked his visits. He tried to mentally subdue them although one tableau after another hurled through his mind forming a collage of Rex shooting up in his truck outside Lisa's house, falling in her living room because he got up to walk without his crutches, handing the kids their sandwiches - bread, forgetting the bologna and mayo. So many stop-ins were ruined. "I had no idea I would miss them so much. I fucked up. I'm doing this for me and them. Shit, I'm their uncle, I'm supposed to be someone they look up to."

During his three-months at the hospital, Rex gained mental clarity and could now, in a word, describe his life for what he thought it had been – squandered. Until now, Rex had been oblivious of the extent to which he had lost his way, and the menace he had truly become. He grew determined to turn his life around and prove to himself, and others, that he could be a productive member of society.

Last Journal Entry

I've been here for 87 days, but who's counting. Tomorrow I go home and I'm scared shitless. Not like I want to stay, because I'm ready to get out of this crazy house, but the thought of facing the music of my bullshit sucks. I could have left any time I wanted, but I chose to stay because I like being clean. I feel so much better. But, fucking Step 9, making amends, I have a lot of

95

those to make. I better write them down so I don't forget. Amends to Ann for living like a pig and selfishly leaving my mess...what a jerk. Amends to Lisa for sure, man I can't wait to see the kids. Wow, I'm getting a second chance to be a positive influence on them. Dad – fuck him! Ah, I'll come back to the list when I get home, it'll give me something to do. Very first thing, find a meeting. I don't want to go through this again.

Rex was going to go home and continue writing. He liked putting his emotions down on paper and felt like he had plenty to say. He wanted to write songs and poetry and use that as an expressive outlet. He even fostered aspirations of becoming a counselor who would help other addicts get clean the way the counselors at the hospital helped him. He had big plans for a better life.

Then it came time to leave the safe, ordinary routine of life at the hospital and go back out into the real world. Rex was clenched with the same fear he felt upon his arrival, though now he was equipped with tools for productive living. Charged with a newfound outlook that overrode his fear, he walked out of the establishment filled with optimism.

At home, Rex planned a weekly meeting schedule and was determined to attend one meeting every day for the first three months of his sobriety. His second day home, he went to a meeting.

11

HOME

Rex took a deep breath and opened the door of his truck in the bank parking lot. His heart ticking like a metronome at 150 beats per minute, armpit sweat flooding down his sides. The first-ever NA meeting he attended was a Thursday lunch meeting, held in a downstairs room at a local bank. The space was the size of a large living room, with dingy white walls, a card table with a tall shiny chrome industrial coffee pot, two short stacks of styrofoam cups, cream, sugar, and stir sticks. About thirty chairs were arranged in a big circle. A large clock hung on the wall next to the door.

Feeling self-conscious, Rex quickly sat down in a chair facing the clock and became preoccupied with not wanting to be noticed. He was aware of people talking in the meeting but didn't hear a word that was said. *Finally 1:30.*

Before Rex could make his escape, a caring lady approached him.

"Hi, I'm Susan. I just want to give you a hug."

"Oh, OK, thank you. I could use one." Susan's soft approach disarmed him.

"I know it's hard, very hard. Is this your first meeting?"

"Uh-huh. I feel like a fish out of water."

"Everyone does their first time. You keep coming back, all right? Susan looked Rex in the eyes. "I want to see you here next week. You're gonna be OK. Just keep coming back."

Rex knew that suggestion was the bedrock to an addict's success in recovery. When an addict finally figures out they cannot remain sober on their own, keep coming back, becomes their life's mantra and is earnestly shared with all newcomers. Those three ordinary words, set forth a radical effect on Rex's psyche. Accustomed to the fact that most people couldn't wait for him to leave, being invited back was foreign to him. Hearing that simple invitation provoked an inner conflict he did not know how to process. He was stuck between being skeptical of her sincerity and truly wanting to believe that she meant what she said.

Hearing the words "keep coming back" also made him acutely aware of the insufferable pain of feeling uncared-for, of how he still had a long road of emotional healing to travel. Despite the fear of this brave new world, he remembered some of the goals he'd set for himself in the hospital; journal, pitch in around the house, complete things he started, keep himself away from his old drug buddies. So he stayed on point and did what the kind-hearted woman requested.

He kept going back.

He obtained a sponsor, made coffee, assisted with setting up the circle of chairs and started to meet a diverse group of people struggling in the same ways he was. Through his visions of becoming a counselor, helping others overcome their addictions, and writing poetry he discovered what it meant to hold a purpose and what it is to have something to strive for. It wasn't long before people enjoyed having him around instead of wanting him to go away. He was beginning to sense that he was welcomed by others, which ever so slightly started to reverse his belief of being unwanted. He was able to walk into a room with the self-assurance of knowing he was sober, and therefore less likely to become a problem. He was welcomed back at his sister's house and for the first time; he played with his niece and nephew as a sober man. His life was moving onward in a positive direction.

Now that Rex was on a mental and emotional upswing, he desired to also improve physically. He initiated the process to get a better fitting prosthetic leg. When Rex was asked to move into the physical rehabilitation center where his leg was being fabricated, so they could customize it properly and train him to walk with it, Rex agreed.

Upon arriving, he felt protected from the pull of his former life; he was in a different town where he did not know anyone and surrounded by health care workers all day. He implemented a safeguard of not leaving the facility, so there was no reason to attend 12-step meetings or bring up the fact that he was a recovering drug addict. On one particularly frustrating morning, while working with his physical therapist, Rex became upset.

"My stump hasn't changed any. Why can't they make me a leg that fits right?" Rex stood next to the exam table concluding he would never get a properly fitted prosthetic leg. One that didn't cause excruciating pain.

"Where is it pinching?" The therapist ran his fingers along the top of the suction cup.

Rex grimaced. "Ouch shit. Yeah, right there on the inner thigh. Same place as always. Take it off, it hurts."

"Hang on, let me make an adjustment."

"Loosening it right there doesn't do anything. It's been tried a hundred times. Just take it off. Fuck this, I'm better with my crutches anyway. It was stupid of me to come here in the first place."

The therapist stood in front of Rex holding his full-length prosthetic leg. "It is heavy, I'll grant you that. Hey, this is a little unconventional, but do you want to go out to my truck and smoke a joint? It'll help you relax."

Coated in the lubricant of exasperation, Rex slid right off the rope of sobriety. "Yes, yes I do."

Rex was not yet able to cope with such high degrees of frustration in a healthy way. He dragged long and slow on the joint, then floated away to that old familiar place of synthetic ecstasy. Instantly the cunning, baffling and powerful disease overtook him and he discarded everything he had been versed in about sobriety.

That night the old lies comforted Rex as he tossed and turned. *I warned you this wouldn't work out. I'm what you need. I'm the only friend you've got. Let's go, it won't be long now until I make you feel better.* The lies hunkered down around him posing like a familiar ally on the battlefield, except they were the enemy closing in on his new belief system and the betrayal convinced him to retreat.

The following morning Rex shoved his unwashed clothes into a half-sized suitcase with one broken latch and gave up the prospect of ever getting a well-fitted prosthetic leg

"Rex, what are you doing? I didn't mean for this to happen," said the physical therapist, who came to check in on Rex.

"Hey, it's cool, I didn't want that leg anyway. It just slowed me down," said Rex as he grabbed his crutches.

"Wait, come on, man. Give it another try."

"It's not your fault. I'm a drug addict." Rex, walked out the door leaving his physical therapist standing there in disbelief.

12

Colorado Rehab

Rex's lapse in judgment hijacked his hopes for a better future. He moved back to Tulsa and picked up right where he left off with his old drug buddies: sleeping on a different couch every night, shooting heroin with dirty needles, living on social security, not caring about anything or anyone except himself.

After several weeks of living at the bottom of his life having very few showers and changes of clothes and again forbidden to see his niece and nephew, a laboring bloom sprouted from the love that was planted at his previous 12-step meetings. The strength of that experience germinated in his frozen soul thawing it just enough for him to recognize he again required correction.

Because his disability insurance paid the cost of rehabilitation centers, while residing in Tulsa, Rex tried a few more times to live sober, each ending in relapse. However, the words "keep coming back" never left him. Because of that, he was able to maintain some friendships made during his regular attendance at Narcotics Anonymous meetings. When he became desperate enough, he could always call his old sponsor, Tom.

Rex met Tom after he completed the program at the psych ward. Tom, a silver-haired handsome take-no-shit kind of man, attended the meeting at the bank, where Rex had been a regular, before he went to be fitted for his prosthetic leg.

It was during the fourth meeting when Rex went to Tom and introduced himself. Tom's cousin who was an amputee and could identify with Rex in that way. That made it easy for Tom to say yes, when Rex asked him to be his sponsor.

Around that time, in a moment of clear thinking, Rex arranged for Tom to manage his money, no longer wanting to involve his sister in his affairs. He asked his sponsor to give him a little at a time for food, gas, and other necessities, which Tom was glad to do. While Rex was away at the physical therapy center, he didn't need money. Therefore, he retained a reserve of social security funds, plus what was left of his accident settlement. In an emergency, he knew right where to go.

One evening on the verge of becoming completely undone, withdrawing from a heroin binge, Rex needed to get high to stave off the dope sickness. Hell-bent on making Tom give him his money, Rex sped straight to Tom's house. Rex visited there before and knew it was the third house on the left with the blue porch light. He screeched up to the curb, pumped and ready to rumble.

Rex marched up to the front porch, his heart pounding, leaned on his crutches for balance and banged on the door with both fists as hard and loud as he could.

"Tom, come out here right now," Rex bellowed at the top of his voice. "Give me my money."

"Hey, check yourself," ordered Tom, who quickly answered the door.

"Man, I gotta get some money. I'm in trouble," Rex pleaded.

"I told you not to come here if you were high, now leave." Tom stepped outside and shut the door.

"You don't understand, man. I'm hurting, here."

"I understand all right, you're the one who doesn't understand. Lower your voice."

"I promise if you give me the money, I will never come here again."

"Shit, Rex, what are you doing, man? Look at yourself," said Tom, who had been in that place himself.

Tom calmed Rex down and listened to his plight. Tom agreed to give him the money but demanded Rex follow him to the bank so Tom could get it from the ATM.

Instead of going to the bank, Tom drove straight to a treatment center with Rex tailing him. He put his car in park, turned the engine off, and braced himself for the wrath he was going to face. Rex pulled in at an angle and abruptly parked his truck. He knew where they were.

"I'm going to kick your ass," Rex yelled, shaking his fist inside the cab of his truck.

"Rex, take it easy," said Tom walking over to Rex.

"I don't know what you think you're doing. Where's my money?"

"Rex, I'm not giving you any money. Now come on, let's go inside."

"You got another thing coming if you think I'm going in there."

"We can stand out here as long as you want. I'm not letting you leave. And, I will kick *your* ass if I have to," said Tom, not backing down.

"Yeah, well, I hope you got all night, cause I do."

"Why don't you go inside?"

After half an hour of negotiating in the parking lot, Tom persuaded Rex to go inside and talk to a counselor. While Rex was in the counselor's office, his sponsor slipped out to the parking lot and let the air out of all four of Rex's truck tires, to ensure he would not be driving in that state of mind and watched the sunset as he waited for Rex to come out.

Because Rex attended N.A. meetings all over town, he and the counselor, Tony, were familiar with each other. Undeterred by the troubled demeanor that wrapped around Rex like a piggy-back ride as he entered the office, Tony looked Rex in the eye and did not drop his gaze until water clouded his sight. Then he spoke.

"Rex, I can't do anything for you here. You are beyond my aide," said the counselor, tears streaming down his cheeks. "If you keep this up you are going to die. It's just that simple."

Rex sat taciturn, as he listened to the genuine concern of the man sitting across from him. He was lanced by the words Tony spoke, knowing they were true.

"There's a more equipped, long-term, treatment center in Colorado. I think you should go there," encouraged Tony. "Rex, it is going to be your best chance at turning your life around."

"Can you tell me about it?" asked Rex, with his head down. Here he was again at the bottom of his life and someone offering to help him up.

"Well, it's near the Rockies in Denver."

Rex perked up when the counselor made the rehab sound more like a spa retreat in the mountains surrounded by pine trees than a drug treatment center. Rex pictured a high altitude paradise and could almost smell the fresh air. He acquiesced without contention.

"Tom, you got a suitcase I can use?" Rex yelled as he came out of the building.

"Hell ya, I do. That's my boy!" Tom slapped Rex on the back and pulled him in for a hug.

"Guess I'm going to Colorado."

"You made the right choice. So, hang tight while I pump up your tires." Tom retrieved an air pump from his vehicle.

"You let the air out of my tires?"

"Yep. I didn't know what the outcome would be, Tom said, and I wasn't going to let you drive in that state of mind and you sure as shit weren't coming to my house."

"You were going to leave me stranded?" Rex looked around at the almost empty parking lot.

"I figured you'd sleep it off in your cab and we could deal with it tomorrow."

"You're an asshole. But, thanks man for being there."

Rex's illusions of freshwater streams and tranquility were abruptly shattered when he was met by Mike and Darren, two muscle-bound dudes with shaved heads, at the Denver airport. Mike's handshake felt like a vice grip on Rex's fingers, causing him to wince. He pretended to lose his balance so he didn't have to shake Darren's hand. Their beefiness bulged through their T-shirts and the crease down the middle of each pant leg notified that they had been pressed. Rex looked down at his long split-ended ponytail draped over his shoulder, bright orange and blue tie-dye T-shirt, torn up blue jeans, and his one Teva sandal. *What have I gotten myself into this time?*

When they arrived at the unkempt property located in a seedy part of downtown Denver, far from any place a deer would roam, the Orderlies put Rex in a small stark room with a few folding chairs and sneered, "Let the games begin." It turned out Rex had a different definition of games than they did.

"You're a worthless piece of shit," they belittled. "A screwup. And you will never amount to anything."

Darren's face so was close to Rex's that his spit landed on Rex's cheeks as the Mr. Clean look-a-like insisted that all Rex would ever be was a "leeching-off-society drug addict."

Rex understood their technique of breaking people down, but he already felt worthless; he didn't need anyone to get in his face and remind him. Rex didn't want to stay. With nowhere else to go, it was his only choice.

Rex called the group sessions group shoutings. At times he would chuckle over the absurdity of it and did his best to stifle the sound for fear of being heard and prolonging the verbal barrage. It all reminded him of the brimstone and fire church services he and his brother were made to sit through as children. The preacher pacing across the riser, spit flying as his voice raised and lowered in passionate anger. "Repent from your wicked ways or burn in hell." He would get scolded for fidgeting, then start giggling after his mother told him to hush. He couldn't stop himself even though he knew what awaited him at home: the fury of his dad.

Treatment Center staff were forbidden to cause physical harm to patients, no matter how much they were provoked. Safe from beatings, Rex soon became indifferent to his daily tongue-lashings.

The intensity of the breaking down phase eased after a couple of weeks and Rex settled into the daily rehab routine: Three square meals, group sessions, private sessions, chores and some free time. During his leisure time, he would traipse around the pavement and small dirt area at the back of the facility. He counted ninety steps to cross the yard. Halfway across he would get angry, thinking about the way he felt duped into being under the impression he was going to the mountains. Instead of freshwater streams and pine trees, he sought solace plodding back and forth across an ugly square of blacktop and weeds. By the third trip across, his anger would subside and he would be glad he was alone and away from the constant drama of addicts. He knew this place was better than his life in Tulsa.

Late one night he awoke to the sound of shattering glass and people yelling. Curious, he went to see what the commotion was about. In the common area, one of the patients was holding a broken lamp. The man had removed the shade and broke the base to produce a jagged ceramic edge. Jutting it forward, he was threatening to kill anyone who came near him. Rex, unfazed by the situation, stood poised ready to use his crutches as weapons if required, kept a safe distance standing next to a manager. He overheard her say that his visitor earlier in the day must have snuck him something, and she was going to call the orderlies.

One by one, all the people in Rex's section gathered around to watch the theatrics. It was very tense as the patient, in a frenzy, kept waving the broken lampstand, likely to lunge at the first person to make a move. Finally, the shout squad barreled through the entry doors and without blinking, double-teamed the guy, seized the lamp and carried him away by his pants. That was the first and only time Rex was glad to see Mike and Darren. Relieved nobody was hurt and not too much damage occurred, the night supervisor took charge. "OK everyone, shows over, back to bed. Come on, no lingering in the halls. Back to bed."

Rex's experience at this treatment center wasn't unlike any of the other programs he had been through, just longer. After eight months he tired of the confinement and boredom of rehab life. He felt he learned again how to live sober and had taken advantage of all that was recommended. The treatment center in his mind had nothing left to offer him, so why should he stay. There was government-subsidized housing not far from the center in downtown Denver that some of the other addicts transitioned to when their year was up. Rex could afford a small room and waited for a spot to open up. When space became available, he resolved to bank on fate, and walked out of the treatment center feeling like a free man leaving jail.

He should have stayed.

13

ONE MORE TRY

In less than forty-eight hours Rex found the nearest dealer, scored meth, caused disruption in the transition home and got himself kicked out. On the sordid streets of west Denver, he frittered away the daylight hours on a plot of land in the middle of the street, in front of the Rescue Mission where he now slept dreamless nights on a worn-out mattress. The scheming demon of addiction tricked and pillaged his mind once again, leaving a ravaged carcass of defeat.

At the intersection of Park Ave., West and Lawrence, Broadway crosses the two streets diagonally north-east to south-west, producing a triangle in the middle of the boulevard.

Triangle Park, a mangy island bordered with sidewalks and metal benches, sits in that junction. Sparse of grass and trees it is insufficient to hold joyfully the bounty of aimless dwellers. Desolate, Rex became a fixture there, fat, disoriented, disheveled and missing his front teeth.

It was house rules at the Mission, that the guests make their beds each morning before they leave. Rex stretched his sheets tight the way he was taught in the Navy, pulled the thinning bedcover over his pillow and smoothed out any visible wrinkles. Sometimes he and the fellow next to him, also a veteran, would eyeball each other's bed to make sure it would pass military inspection. On this morning after Rex passed his bunk mate's scrutiny, he searched the pockets of his blue jeans and scraped up enough change to buy two bottles of Night Train Express. The other homeless winos and he referred to Night Train as the bum wine and drank it for the sole purpose of escaping their forsaken lives. Ready to start his day, Rex stopped at the liquor store one block away and bought two bottles.

Rex hobbled to his spot, slumped down on the curb at Park Ave., West, in front of Triangle Park and carefully opened the first bottle of wine as if it were a delicate flower, needing to be handled gingerly. The colorful label brought back childhood memories of him and his brother when they lived in the house with the big shade tree in the front yard.

"Hello friend," he wearily whispered, and pressed the cool bottle against his cheek.

Slowly bringing the NightTrain to his lips, Rex tipped it up and indulged in a long, slow drink. The harshness of the alcohol ironically left a warm trail of satisfaction as it ran down his throat and passed through his insides. Similar to when he was a young boy in Arkansas, sneaking swigs of whiskey from his dad's collection, it comforted him. He knew that at least for a little while he would be all right.

Halfway through the first bottle, just as he felt his body start to relax, a policeman on a motorcycle pulled up and stopped in front of him. Rex tried to avoid looking at him, but, regrettably, they made eye contact.

"You drinking out here on the street?" quizzed the cop.

"Yes, sir. Just one small sip, but I was going to put the lid back on," stammered Rex.

"It's against the law to be drinking on the street."

"Yes, sir. I am putting it away right now." Rex picked the lid up off of the dusty sidewalk.

"You're going to have to give me that bottle." The officer reached his hand out.

117

"No, sir. I am putting it away right now," rebutted Rex as he fumbled putting the bottle back into the brown paper bag.

"Give me that," said the policeman, as he yanked the bottle from Rex's hand. The officer confiscated the open container, turned it upside down, and poured the wine into the gutter at Rex's foot. Then he opened the second, tipped it over and spilled the contents down the run-off drain.

As the wine hit the ground, Rex saw it splash back up and sparkle crimson in the sunlight as it danced its way onto him, leaving a stain of red dots on the leg of his tattered blue jeans. The most important ingredient of his day, what he cared for like a newborn child just moments before vanished in an instant. His life's sustenance flowed down the sewer mixed with the dirt, trash, and grime.

When the officer was finished emptying all the Night Train, he ordered Rex to, "Move away from the curb." Dejected from the confrontation, Rex stood up, steadied himself on his crutches as best he could, and like a beaten dog limped over to the nearest rusting bench, where he curled up in a stupor of hopelessness for the remainder of the day. The voices of previous counselors ricocheted through his mind.

"Rex, the odds of you getting and staying clean are in the bleakest statistical category." "The young age at which you became addicted and the subsequent life traumas you endured, stack the recovery deck against you like a mountain that can't be scaled." "Rex, you don't even have a high school diploma." "Most people don't make it out of your stage of addiction with its insurmountable odds." While tumbling down the black hole of his shattered spirit an unexpected light flickered in the distance.

Far down, in a hidden room of his heart, he sensed there was more for him. A barely detectable voice was begging for him to trust that he could live a sober meaningful life, that his story would inspire other hopeless people. The small voice urged him to not give up, and the memory of the kind lady who told him to keep coming back after his first N.A. meeting gave him the courage to try sobriety again. More than ever before, after experiencing a genuine rock bottom, he grasped that if he continued on this path, held captive at the fringes of society, it would surely lead to death. He did not want to die, not like this, alone in a treeless park or an alleyway in a town where nobody knew him. Clenching to the remote possibility of personal significance, he was able to muster up enough energy to try rehab one more time.

While staying nights at the Rescue Mission, he heard about a program at a local VA center that was available to anyone who served in the military, regardless of the duration.

The program would authorize people to live at the VA facility as long as they were looking for a job, clean and sober and obeying house rules. After his encounter with the motorcycle cop at Triangle Park, he opted to inquire about it.

The next morning he obtained the address from the Mission manager. It was the spring of 1984, the crisp air pricked his ear lobes as he walked the few blocks to the halfway house. Rex stood in front of the dingy white door defaced with graffiti, concluding that the writing said: "you suck." He went in and sat on one of the three folding chairs in the drab lobby. It was quiet except for the music playing on the other side of the wall, "Sometimes love don't feel like it should…" A man that looked to be the same age as Rex, came out singing, "Hurt so good. And so good it is. Well hello there sad face, that must be why you're in this place. Oh, don't mind me."

"Are there any beds, asked Rex?"

The administrator made it very clear that this was a halfway house to help struggling veterans integrate into the working world. Weekly urinalysis tests would be given, and if they came up dirty there would be consequences. It was nicer than sleeping at the Mission, so Rex checked in.

Rex lived at that transition house for two weeks. During that time he turned in three urinary analysis tests and all three

UI's were dirty. After the first UI was bad he gave up and decided to take advantage of the free food and shelter as long as he could. It became merely a place where he could eat a hearty meal and have a hot shower. At the end of those two weeks, after producing three dirty UI tests, the staff ceased to be sympathetic and told him that he could no longer stay at the half-way house. He tried to muster up an attitude, that would momentarily protect him from his pain, this time he couldn't. The energy required to strut out the door with a big "fuck you" chip on his shoulder eluded him. It was just another notch of failure.

How many times would he try to kick his addiction to drugs and alcohol only to end up the same disappointment he felt he had always been? Rex wondered why people were inclined to continue giving him another chance, knowing about all his futile attempts to stay sober. He couldn't make heads or tails of it when, instead of throwing him back into the trenches, the half-way house administrator sent him to an in-house VA treatment center.

Consumed by despair, he went through the motions of another standard intake routine, and filling out the same necessary paperwork. As he was looking down at the address section on the application, he wrote in Triangle Park as his last place of residence, then scratched it out. Faus, the old man

121

assisting him piped up. "Great! Rex, you're set up in room 14, bed A." Faus tucked his long gray hair behind his ears.

"You should give that bed to someone you can help, because you can't help me. Nobody can help me," Rex mumbled without looking up. "My addiction is worse, no matter how hard I try I use again. I've been through a lot of rehabs. People yelled at me and hugged me. I'm sure some wanted to punch me in the face. All the group therapy and counselors, none of it worked, none and neither will this one."

The counselor sympathized, "That does appear to be the case, Rex, and I don't know if what we do here will be any different than what you did at other treatment centers. I can't give you a guarantee, what I will say is this: The sun is shining, it's 75 degrees with a slight breeze. It's a perfect day to be enjoying the outdoors. I would like to be playing on the slide with my grandkids at the park in my neighborhood. I'm sure it is the same beautiful day at Triangle Park if you would rather go back there. And, Rex, your addiction is no worse than anybody else's."

The compassion in his eyes and lines on his leathery face signaled to Rex that the old man understood his despair. Rex blankly stared at him as his mind tried to reconcile a beautiful day and Triangle Park. It couldn't. With a lump in his throat, Rex looked back down at the application, skipped over the address section, and fighting back tears of unworthiness, finished the forms.

"Good choice there, Rex," acknowledged the counselor. "You know, we're making an exception for you."

"You are?"

"Usually you have to be in the military a year to get in here. We are making an exception because of your disability."

"I didn't have my accident in the Navy."

"That's all right," the counselor smiled and fiddled with his nameplate that read "Faus Man."

Even if it was a perfect day weather-wise, Rex could not go back to Triangle Park. He could never go back to Triangle Park. "Thank you," said Rex, as he resolutely slid his completed forms across the desk, to the counselor.

As with all the other treatment centers Rex had been, this one had its group sessions and private sessions, and it also held N.A. meetings at the facility during the week. All the inpatients were required to attend as part of the treatment.

Rex listened to the people talking about how much the program has done for them. How they didn't know where they would be without it. The Pollyanna attitude of some of the attenders caused Rex's temper to flare.

"This is a fucking waste of time," Rex shouted when it was his turn. "This program is shit and you can't tell me it's not," he yelled, trembling with rage. "This is all bullshit. These meetings have done nothing but waste my time. This has never worked for me, ever!" Rex screamed at the group, veins bulging from his forehead.

Still, at the end of the night when the meeting was over, people came up to Rex and introduced themselves, shook his hand and said those three enchanting words, "Keep coming back."

It was during those meetings that a new awareness started chipping away at Rex's pride. After the way he treated the members, it was humbling to Rex for people in this group to come and tell him they wanted him to keep coming back. Rex finally adopted a truth he had for so long denied; He didn't possess the fortitude to stay clean by himself, even for one day.

This time, at the end of yet another month in treatment, he, at last, gained respect for the level of commitment required to live sober; meetings every day, accountability partners, no longer believing the lie of *just this once* and accepted step one of the 12 Steps. "We admitted we were powerless over our addiction - that our lives had become unmanageable."

Although he felt more assured than ever before about his chance at living clean, he made up his mind to place no expectation on his future or his sobriety.

14

BUS RIDE

The bulging duffle bag included just enough room in the outside compartment for a shoe and notebook after Rex stuffed his toiletries, the two T-shirts he'd gotten from the donation bin at the rescue mission, his other pair of jeans, beanie, and winter jacket into the carrier. He completed the twenty-eight-day VA treatment program.

Rex had just zipped up his bag when Trinket, well, Teddy, who wasn't at all dainty like the name suggests, walked in.

"Hey Rex, I made you something."

"Yeah?"

"It's not much. Here." Trinket handed Rex a rock.

As Rex rubbed his thumb across the brown and grey stone, his skin caught on the V that Trinket carved into it.

"The V stands for victory because that's what we're going to be this time, Rex, victorious!"

"Thanks, man. I appreciate this."

"Out in the world, I was alone and forgotten. I can't go through life like that again." The words that Trinket spoke seared Rex. "I know it's just a rock from the yard. I hope you'll keep it and remember ol' Trinket when you look at it."

Rex stored the rock in his pocket. "Hey Teddy, you're going to be fine. Just keep doing what you're doing."

Rex went and found Jackson, the rehab comedian, famous for his silly knock-knock jokes and being the resident food critic.

"Hey Rex, knock-knock."

"I don't know man, you got me good last time. I just came to say bye."

"Nah, come on man, for old-time sake? This one's good." Jackson convinced Rex to play along. "Knock-knock."

"OK. Who's there?"

"Betchu."

"Betchu who?"

"Bet you can't tell me what we ate for lunch yesterday." Rex laughed more at Jackson being proud of himself than the joke.

"Good point, I'm going to say casserole, but who knows?"

Rex made the rounds and said tearful goodbyes to the people who became his real allies in their front on addiction. Together they crawled through the trenches of false pride, humiliation, and snot-producing sobs. For twenty-eight days they vowed that when a comrade was down, that person would be protected by a Flack jacket of people who cared.

Faus, his counselor, was a protective shield, who provided aide to Rex as he progressed in his recovery. His advice enabled Rex to break through to a greater stratum of honesty about his self-destructive behavioral patterns. Faus helped Rex begin to accept that his own choices and attitudes perpetuated his years of active using.

"Today's the day, huh?" Faus sipped his coffee.

"Yeah, my bags packed and ready to go." Rex gestured down the hall toward his room.

"Sit down for a minute, Rex."

During that final stay in treatment, with the guidance of his counselor, Rex came out of denial enough to admit that he truly could not stay clean without the guidance of a higher power. He also shed enough of his pride to know that even one drink would send him spiraling back to that path of madness which would ultimately steer him to death. He felt indebted to his counselor, and his payback would be to stay clean.

"I never told you why I'm called Faus."

"That's not your name?"

"My real name is Brent. I got the nickname Faucet early in my addiction because my mouth was always running and there was a steady stream of addicts flowing through my house. I was proud of that nickname. I thought it was cool."

Rex listened as Faus imparted that one day an alteration took place in him, similar to what Rex was experiencing. A true change.

"At first I wanted to get rid of the name so I didn't have that constant reminder."

"Why didn't you?"

"Because it still fits. I have addicts in and out of my life, and I always have something to say. What started as uncomplimentary, has become my greatest privilege. It's been an honor for me to work with you, Rex. Come and see me anytime."

Rex was by no means a healed and whole man, however, the shift the counselor observed was enough for him to vouch for Rex. Faus talked to the house manager at the transitional home Rex had been kicked out of and arranged for him to be given another chance. Faus also told Rex where there was a meeting he could go to that evening.

As Rex waited for the bus that would take him to the meeting, he alternated between looking out the window that faced the boulevard and looking at the clock on the wall in the lobby area, the ticking louder with each passing second. A part of him wished the bus wouldn't come and he could go back to Room 14 Bed A and cleave to his safety net.

But, the bus rounded the corner a block down the street, right on time. Rex threw his dark blue duffle bag, crammed with every possession he owned, over his shoulder and walked out to the stop across the road. The driver pulled up in front of him and opened the door. He saluted Rex and with a twinkling smile asked: "How ya doin' today sir?" Rex climbed on the bus, inserted the exact change in the meter, looked at the gentleman and nodded his head.

There was an empty seat near the front where Rex leaned his crutches against the window, sat down and placed his bag beside him on the bench. After rubbing his hand across the worn brown and orange seat fabric, he flicked away a sunflower seed shell, then hunched over and closed his eyes.

Resting his forehead on his wrists, he kept his head down and did not look at any other passengers for fear of losing focus of his single thought: to get to that meeting before he changed his mind.

As new passengers embarked at stops along the way, he heard the clinking of change as they dropped their fares into the tube. It was evident to him that some were regulars on this route because they addressed the bus driver by name and asked how he was doing. His answer was always the same, he would chuckle and say, " Ahhh, you know, jus livin' the dream." One person on the third stop poked back at him and asked, "Is your dream black and white or color?" Hearing the playful banter, Rex wondered what living the dream meant, and if he would ever greet that experience.

He ruminated about all he'd been through and strained to think of something positive, something that could link him to a life dream. He came up empty.

Some good times, though, did come to mind. He remembered fishing at the pond with his brother on sticky summer evenings when they were kids, flirting with cute girls in elementary school and being embarrassed when his face turned blush, the empowerment he felt while water skiing, with one leg, at the lake and being amused by his silly-willy niece and nephew vrooming their toys in the air.

131

The warm series of recollections washed over him and made him smile, albeit meager. For a little while, he transcended time and forgot where he was. Even if it didn't answer his question of having a life dream, the untroubled reprieve was exactly what he needed. The bus stopped again and the clank of the door opening brought him back into the present. He looked at the clock secured above the rearview mirror, twenty minutes had passed.

"Next stop, anybody getting off?" The bus driver yelled out.

"I am. This is my stop," answered Rex.

He slid his arms through his duffle bag straps and hoisted it onto his back. Standing, he could feel his heartbeat quicken as he looked out the open door at the unassuming arena of war. Trembling with uncertainty, he took a deep breath, stepped off the bus and into the first day of the rest of his life. Faus drew him a map from the bus stop to the building. Rex followed it precisely.

Once the building came in to view, Rex sped up his pace wanting desperately to be inside, buffered from temptation. The meeting was his bulletproof vest. The closer he came to the door, the burden of not making it lifted and he began to feel less and less vulnerable. Victory washed over him as he made that last step to the front of the door.

There he found a sign taped to the door that said the meeting was moved to another location. Panic gripped him and with urgency, he fumbled through his bag and found a pen and tablet to scribble down the address. He had been in Denver for a while, but only in treatment centers and Triangle Park. He did not know the names of avenues or his way around. He began to walk aimlessly, not knowing if he was going in the right direction.

Weeping, every tear that rolled down his cheek doused the fire of his new commitment a little more. Knowing he should do something quick, he worked up his courage to ask a woman for directions, "This is the place." Divine guidance took him right to the meeting site.

Drained from the unnerving pilgrimage, he entered the room and collapsed into a chair, relieved that he'd made it. A friendly petite lady, wearing a T-shirt with the quote "It works if you work it," was making coffee. She was the lone person there. It was an hour before the meeting. She welcomed Rex with a big hug. "I'm Patty."

Solaced by the presence of a fellow addict in recovery, he knew he would be safe from self-destruction while he was there.

When the meeting started, the facilitator announced that it was a birthday meeting and explained to the newcomers that when people reached certain points in their sobriety they are recognized with a token. As the chips were being given out for one-month, two-years, ten-years clean, the people in the group were laughing and celebrating their significant accomplishments. It was a joyous time for everyone but Rex, who despite his full battery of hope, was terrified of the world outside.

"What are you people laughing at?" he finally stood up and asked. "You are all laughing and carrying on like this isn't serious. Well, for me it is. I'm dying over here. When I walk out that door, the bet's off for me. I don't know what I'll do and I'm scared to death," Rex lamented, his voice cracking. He sat back down shaking and a little embarrassed to have exposed himself so personally his first time there.

The other attendees were drawn to his rawness. At the end of the meeting, many approached Rex and fortified him with words of encouragement.

"Thanks for sharing man, I know it's hard," said one person.

"I know how it is, I've been there. You're at the right place now," said another.

"Just keep it real and soon you'll be getting a chip, too," another person said.

People from the group gave him their phone numbers, and, of course, told him to "keep coming back." He received fifteen telephone numbers that night. There were too many emotions simultaneously swirling around in his heart and head to do anything more than say, "Thank you." It happened so fast that he couldn't sort out exactly what was going on. Somehow he knew they were serious, and not just following protocol for when down and out newcomers attend.

One phone number belonged to Patty, who had been setting up refreshments when he first walked in. Like others in the group, she told him to "keep coming back." However, that was not all she advised him. In a stern, almost scolding tone she said, "Rex, I'll tell you what to do if you want to stay clean. You'll not only keep coming back, you'll also call those numbers. Think of those phone numbers as your lifeline to sobriety, and no matter how bad you don't want to, pick up the phone and make a call."

When he curled up in bed that night and thought about the meeting, he realized it wasn't the other people being serious about their concern for him that was different. He was different. He closed his eyes and slept peacefully through the night.

Rex made the phone calls like he was told and the Tuesday night group became his new family and a man named Stan his sponsor.

"If we're going to do this Rex, there will be no bullshit, understood?" stated Stan.

"Whoa, what am I getting myself into here?"

"I mean it. I've seen too many guys go down before their time because they wouldn't do the work."

"If I wanted to die, Stan, I'd already be dead."

"You ever work the steps before?"

"Yeah, of course, I have."

"Then why are you just getting out of Rehab again, Rex?"

"All right already! Just tell me what you want me to do."

During their weekly accountability meetings, Rex became more transparent than ever before. He shared with Stan that although he believed in and relied upon a divine source, he still struggled with defining clearly what that meant. He told him that his first exposure to God had been through hypocritical, fundamentalist religious family members who acted piously at church on Sunday, then behaved wickedly Monday through Saturday.

Rex shared it was because of that phoniness he developed a strong disdain for organized religion and a looming mistrust of God. Shifting his perspective toward The Almighty as a force who represented goodness and love was difficult and slow going. "I prayed to God this week," Rex told Stan.

136

"So how was that?"

"Weird. It was weird."

Rex ultimately viewed his fellow recovery comrades as his higher power. They were the people who lived the same way every day of the week. They were friends he could count on. They were the folks who embraced him and liked having him around. He was surrounded by people who inspired him and gave him hope. He subscribed to the notion that being a part of something consistent and healing could restore him to sanity – that and doing what he was told.

Finally, he no longer retained the urge to travel that old dismal route, of strung-out and, whatever the cost, would do anything to stay clean. The recovery seeds planted in him from all of his previous attempts at sober living began to break through and overtake the deeply embedded weeds of active addiction. That prepared his inner self for a spiritual awakening, the key ingredient in step two of the 12 steps to recovery: "We came to believe that a Power greater than ourselves could restore us to sanity."

The group and meeting with Stan were the main staples in Rex's fragile life. He went faithfully and did everything his sponsor told him to do. Stan would be the catalyst to the second most significant turning point in Rex's life.

15

SNOW SKIING

An avid snow skier, Stan invited Rex to go skiing with a group of friends. Except for a few water skiing trips in Tulsa, Rex had not thought about sports in years. He had been athletically inclined as a teenager, however, since his accident the likelihood of being active eluded him. He agreed to Stan's invitation, figuring he didn't have much to lose.

Early one Saturday morning, they loaded their misfit selves into the truck. When the last door was pulled shut, much to Rex's chagrin, the teasing began.

"You shouldn't have worn jeans, Rex, those will be soaked within the first five minutes," one person joked.

"Did you bring plenty of sunscreen? We wouldn't want your pretty little nose to get sunburned," another person jabbed.

"Your gloves look like something I would wear for gardening," someone else wisecracked.

"Rex we're giving you shit because we love you, man. You know that right?" Stan asked.

"I know. Just wait till my one-legged ass out skis your pansy ass." Rex razzed back.

On and on the bantering went, the home-group comfortably stowed inside the warm vehicle as they whizzed up the steep, winding, snow-edged highway.

The farther into the mountains they ascended, the dense snow twinkled brighter as the sun's rays reflected off the untouched blanket of powder, giving the appearance of spring, though it was a bitter-cold winter day. Mesmerized by nature, Rex was staring out the window when it dawned on him that maybe his comrades weren't joking. He shouldn't have worn jeans!

A momentary annoyance bubbled up inside of Rex as it registered, that it would have been courteous of somebody to let him borrow a pair of waterproof ski pants. He rejected the intruder, and did not let it set up camp in his mind, refusing to let the suggestion develop into a mood that would ruin his day. The worst thing that could happen, he thought, was that his pants would become wet and freeze. So what! He was on an adventure with his new friends, hanging out in the ultimate that nature offered. Reposed in his new attitude, he observed how much more enjoyable his life was now that he could choose his state-of-mind. He resumed gazing at his surroundings and began to weep.

"I get it, man," said Stan, who glancing in the rearview mirror noticed Rex's silent tears.

"I'm just overwhelmed right now," Rex whispered, wiping his wet cheeks on his sleeve. "I feel small, you know, but in a good way."

"When the haze is gone everything is more potent. Soak it up my friend there is nothing more spiritually formidable than nature." Stan used the moment to teach his new student.

The group sat quietly for the rest of the drive, in an impromptu separate, and collective meditation.

At Winter Park ski resort, Stan spotted a parking space at the end of the gravel lot. Somewhat late in the morning, all the stalls closest to the staging area were taken. The moment the truck engine was turned off, right on queue as if choreographed and rehearsed a hundred times, the doors flew open and Rex's buddies departed the vehicle. They put on their down feather jackets and began the production of unloading. The skis were pulled out first and leaned against the side of the 4-wheel drive, then the boots. After that came the snack baggies full of nuts and beef jerky, to be stored in zippered pockets inside their coats. Finally, everyone pulled thickly knit beanies over their ears and donned their Oakley sunglasses. Rex, conspicuous about being the new guy, stayed out of the way.

"We'll put our boots on at the lockers," Stan said, handing Rex his gear.

At last, it was time to make the trek toward the ski lift. The uncertainty of what would come made Rex reflect upon other first walks he had taken: His initial steps with one leg, the traipse to the detox desk at the psychiatric hospital, and the plod across the parking lot at the bank where he attended his first-ever N.A. meeting. This walk, he noticed, was different: he wasn't infused with defeatism. The thin high-altitude air, the two packs of cigarettes a day he smoked for ten years, and the seventy extra pounds he'd packed on since his accident, highlighted another stark contrast from the other walks. He was exhausted and needed to sit down. He was unaware of just how out of shape he had become but concluded the discomfort of squashing his stomach while bending down to remove his

141

tennis shoe, was better than the life-depleting addiction he had been in for way too many years.

Looking at the chimney stack from the Lodge's fireplace as it jetted toward the heavens while smoke plumed out of its mouth, Rex imagined it called out to him to enjoy the day as he watched the skiers through the gigantic picture window that faced the slopes. He knew there was no way he was going to be able to make it out to the ski lift. There was also no way his friends were going to let him weasel out of the day's activities by drinking hot cocoa and lounging on an overstuffed sofa inside the resort.

"Rex here comes your ride," said Stan.

"The snowmobile?"

"Yeah, I arranged for you to get a ride up."

"You must be Rex," said the driver, his teeth shone white against his tan face.

"That's me," answered Rex, seeing his reflection in the drivers mirrored goggles.

"Hop on and lay the ski across your lap." Rex did as told and again became acutely aware of his gut.

"Where we going?" The driver asked Stan.

"The Bunny Slope."

"Did you have to say it that way?" Rex admonished Stan.

Rex sat on the back of the snowmobile and Stan laid Rex's ski and poles across his lap. "Don't lose these."

"Hold on to the side handles," the driver revved the engine.

"Take all the time you want, go the long way. How about we get a tasty hot chocolate instead?" Rex kidded to the driver.

"Nice try pal. I'll see you up there," said Stan.

"I'll have him at the lift in about ten minutes." The driver sped off.

Not fully recuperated from the long walk, Rex knew he was in trouble and questioned his agreement to go along for this fun day on the mountain, except there was no turning back now. It was go time on the Bunny Slope.

Stan hooked Rex's boot into the ski. A lump of anxiety clogged his throat as Rex realized he was in way over his head. This was across the universe from sitting on his couch with the television remote, eating Hagen Daaz ice cream out of the carton. With the proper apparatus now locked in place, ski poles in hands, and two big dudes at his sides, he summoned the courage to lean forward and stood up.

The snowmobile driver carried on, his helpers let go, and he fell down with a mighty *thunk*. Flecks of snow whirled up around him like he was in a Christmas globe being shaken to make the snow rise and swirl. Without the advantage of the

143

snowmobile seat, it was almost impossible for Rex to stand back up. After five-minutes of grappling with the snow, as predicted in the car ride up, his jeans were soaked.

"Rex, roll onto your side and push up from there," instructed Stan, as he watched Rex plop in the snow again.

"Can't you see that's what I'm trying to do?" Rex rebuked, as he wormed onto his side.

"There, that's it. Now plant your poles and push with your arms," directed Stan, while laughing at Rex's predicament. "You look like Humpty Dumpty on a ski."

For two hours Rex stood up and fell down, his friends couldn't keep themselves from laughing at the scene and even more at Rex's frustration. Trying very hard to ski and not succeeding, Rex's discouragement reached its peak and he struggled with the decision to throw in the towel. He was not a quitter. He resolved for that day, all he needed to do was get to the bottom of the hill. He turned his ski sideways, hoisted himself up, and looked down the slope.

His sponsor, who was a little further down the hill, mischievously decided it would be a good time to throw a snowball at Rex.

Stan packed the snowball and side-armed it at Rex. It beaned him on the left side of his head and exploded into a puff of cold dust. Rex's exasperation turned to fury. "Damn you, I'm going to kick your ass," Rex yelled as he took off with a vengeance. That was the last straw for him, and in his anger, a whole new motivation for skiing burst forth.

"Oh, yeah? Try to catch me," ribbed Stan.

Rex chased after his friend and, much to his surprise, without trying, he was skiing and it was glorious.

He wasn't thinking about what he was doing, so his body did not tense up – it stayed relaxed and agile. To his surprise, his knee acted like a shock absorber, rising and bending with the terrain, rather than like a wooden log resisting every turn and mogul. He zoomed fast enough and far enough for the wind to chap his cheeks, and a smile plastered itself on his face. He felt free and victorious. It turned out to be one of the most beautiful days of his life and the first of many outings to come.

Within a few months and several lessons through the disabled skiers training class, Rex became competent in gliding down the North face of Winter Park. At the end of his first year of snow skiing, he was a member of the disabled racing team and had also become a volunteer for the National Sports Center for the Disabled (NSCD). Passionate about skiing, he taught others the sport, too.

Rex's opportunity to assist others in overcoming their obstacles, to live with fulfillment and vitality, was satisfying an abandoned desire. A forgotten dream that dared to peek into his life during his very first stay in a treatment facility. His not-so-distant-past of being a homeless wino living in a downtown park was hard to imagine. He truly had turned a corner and was now experiencing life from new and healthy perspectives

16

STEP THREE

As Rex tackled the slopes of the Rocky Mountains, he noticed his physical body was changing and adapting to the more rigorous lifestyle of an active person. He dismissed his slothful ways, put down the cigarettes and started to shed the excess 70 pounds. The outward change was a manifestation of what was happening to him on the inside, a sloughing off of a worn-out coat that told a story of a life gone wrong. Its frayed edges and torn seams would always be remembered; they served Rex as a reminder of where he came from, a place he vowed never to go back to. At the dawn of a paradigm shift, he wrestled with a new possibility: That perhaps it was his self-centeredness and not God's abandonment, that was the cause of his problems. He was ready to refashion his identity physically, mentally and spiritually.

The turbulent waters that once tossed him to and fro subsided; his trust in the group as a higher power was helping to keep him above water. It was time to plunge headfirst into the depths of Step 3: "Made a decision to turn our will and our lives over to the care of God, as we understood Him."

Conquering Step 3 would prove to be the toughest battle in his war to stay clean. The pervasive, bullying voice of his stinging childhood was hindering the way to true serenity. Embracing his support group as his higher power was one thing. Turning his will and life over to God was a whole other matter. It required that he perceive God as someone good, caring, and loving. Rex would have to surrender to a God he was convinced had forsaken him.

He questioned God: "Where were you the night I was molested? Where were you when I had my accident? Where were you, God, when I lived in Triangle Park?"

As far as Rex was concerned, God was nowhere to be seen. However, he kept searching, he kept skiing and through that doggedness, he awakened to the presence of God.

17

BICYCLING

Rex blushed when a friend, Jay, told him he should model for the new marketing brochure he was developing for the Community Care Center, an inpatient treatment facility for mentally disabled young adults. *Wow, I just got my teeth fixed last week and it's already making a difference.* Sobriety, competitive skiing, and now modeling, in awe of what was going on in his life, Rex did what he was told and unexpected opportunities continued to manifest.

Dr. Bruno, founder of the Community Care Center, upon hearing laughter outbursts from Rex and Jay during the photoshoot, dropped in to see what was so funny and how the brochure was coming along.

A middle-aged man of average build, glasses and thick dark hair, Dr. Bruno chuckled too, when Jay showed him the outtake pictures captured when Rex wasn't ready or when he was making a silly face. Dr. Bruno was pleased with the improved circular and liked Rex right away.

"Rex, I hear you are a pretty good handyman," said Dr. Bruno.

"Yeah, better than a model and I don't have to suck in my gut," said Rex, patting, his now much smaller, belly.

"Well, I could use someone like you."

"I can fix just about anything."

"There's not a lot, but enough to keep busy one or two days a week."

"Are you offering me a job?"

"Yes, I am."

Responsible for minor repairs throughout the facility, Rex dealt with each task seriously and completed them in a timely manner. While he was on the premises, he made a point to acquaint himself with the staff and to always say hello to Dr. Bruno. As he proved himself to be reliable, Dr. Bruno added to his responsibilities. He gave Rex more hours by integrating him into the clinical side of the operation.

"Rex, I think you are ready to work hands-on with the patients. It wouldn't be an official counselor capacity, more like a mentor. With your background, you have a lot to offer them. There is one condition; you finish school and get your GED."

"I would love that. For a long time now, I have felt like it's what I'm supposed to do. You know, give support to other addicts. Yes, I will get my GED. Thank you."

Dr. Bruno paired him with those who were also slaves to addiction, and Rex gladly accepted the duty of escorting them to meetings and shared his testimony every chance he could. Thus, a path opened for him to turn his reignited dream, to help suffering people live better, into a way of life.

He loved the one-on-one mentoring sessions with patients at the Center. "What do you mean you don't know? Sure you know. What happened?" Rex knew if he asked one more time, 16-year-old Joe would summon the courage to say what upset him.

"Well, it's embarrassing. I threw a tantrum when my mom said I couldn't go to the movies." Joe fiddled with the bottom button on his shirt. "I threw a plate on the floor and it shattered." As Joe kept talking, his body relaxed. "I didn't mean to do it." Joe looked up at his mentor.

"Sometimes we just snap." Rex jotted notes down in Joe's file. "Just remember, we make our own choices. Why do you think that made you so angry?"

"I don't know, maybe because I didn't get my way, or maybe because she doesn't trust me." Joe dropped his gaze and began, again, to fiddle with his buttons.

"Hey, look at me." Rex reiterated that it was his stealing and lying that caused her distrust. "We'll keep working on it, OK? It took me a long time to be able to control my emotions. It's good that you know why you got so angry." Rex praised him for his self-awareness and told him to give his mother a break.

"Yeah, so that's better than before," Joe said, realizing his growth.

Rex had a way with the patients, instilling respect and value in them, inspiring them to think about bigger possibilities, to see what they could not, and thus, became a genuine change agent. Even as he continued to oversee the building maintenance, Rex became the vocational director for the center. He chaperoned gatherings on day trips to the mountains and the recreation center, and he coordinated school programs and vocational services for patients who required those types of guidance.

Rex's income went from supplementing his monthly disability check to surpassing it. It hadn't been that way since before his accident. Now, he earned enough money to support himself. He was good at fixing things, possessed a knack for carpentry, and he didn't need two legs to do either of those.

Assured about his future at the Community Care Center and his ability to hold down a job, he entertained the idea of canceling his disability allotment. The notion was frightening: for years he relied on his monthly check. Living on disability was safe and secure – no matter what, he could always count on that money coming in. While using drugs, he occasionally worked for cash, although, he never considered giving up the safety net.

With sober eyes, he figured out how being reliant on this sure money was keeping him from trying harder. He saw that he had been bound to a comfort zone that offered no stimulation and roused no passion. Living that way served him well for a long time. Now, maybe, there was a more commendable way. He sought guidance from Dr. Bruno about what to do.

"Rex, I'm impressed with you. You're very industrious and creative. I think you'll do well for yourself," said Dr. Bruno.

"It's scary, you know? I guess I can reapply if things don't work out. I don't want to, though. Once I'm done, that's it."

"It's good that you're struggling with this, it's a big decision. Think about it for a while and keep weighing the pros and cons. Rex, you're quite an entrepreneur and I think you can do it. Just know that you're loved and appreciated as a vital member of our team," counseled Dr. Bruno.

Relying on Dr. Bruno's input, Rex leaped to financial independence, and moved from subsidized housing to renting a room from Skeeter, a recovery friend, who was a regular on the ski trips. One pleasant spring morning Rex and his roommate were tinkering around the yard discussing how Rex should find a way to stay in shape during the offseason of snow skiing.

"Hey, Rex, how about cycling?" Skeeter said gesturing toward the old yellow Huffy bicycle leaning against the paint chipped rail that framed the front porch.

"Funny! You want me to ride that bike?"

"Yeah, why the hell not? Shit, you ski with one leg!"

"Come on!" said Rex, with an incredulous sigh.

"Stay where you are, I'll be right back," said Skeeter hustling inside the house.

"Oh, no," thought Rex, afraid of what Skeeter was up to.

Skeeter came out of the house holding an outstretched leather strap. He tugged on it twice causing the hide to make a loud snap. With great enthusiasm and a hint of mischief, he hooted, "I think this'll do the trick."

Rex didn't like his use of the word *trick* at that moment because he knew the trick was going to be on him.

Skeeter snatched up the rusted mountain bike with one hand while the belt dangled from the other. He rolled the bike alongside Rex's white truck and leaned it against the passenger side of the bed. He looked over at Rex and commanded, "Get up. Let's do this."

Rex laid his crutches in the bed of the truck and held onto the ridge of the truck bed for balance as Skeeter assisted him up onto the bicycle seat. It was surprisingly easy, Rex noticed, since there was no leg to lift up and over the bar. When Rex was steadied on the tiny seat pad, Skeeter bent down and strapped Rex's foot to the peddle using the belt he retrieved from inside the house.

Skeeter gave Rex a running push down the driveway, and Rex began to pedal. His mind remembered how to ride a bike from his childhood days, but his body was no longer the same. It couldn't follow the instructions his brain was commanding. Lopsided and wobbly, he was not at all

155

confident. However, he kept pedaling with his one leg and somehow managed to get to the end of the block, turn himself around, and pedal back to his yard. Immediately upon riding onto the thick grass, Rex lost his balance and fell over, his foot still tied to the pedal.

"Well, that was one way to stop yourself!" said Skeeter, doubled over from a side-splitting howl.

"Help me up, dammit!"

"Next time, pull back up to the truck and grab a hold of the ridge the way you did when you started."

"Now you tell me. Asshole!"

Rex felt in his gut that day that something big was going to happen. It was a mystical intuitive sense that he couldn't put into words. All Rex grasped was that he had it and it was too strong to deny. A dream was born. He fell in love with cycling that afternoon and rode that old tarnished yellow Huffy every day.

He stayed around the neighborhood at first, then expanded his perimeter to the evening N.A. meetings. As his stamina and nerve grew, he ventured out farther and farther. With his one leg, he proudly rode that bike.

Bicycling

A few months after he uncovered his zest for biking, Rex was riding down a descent in downtown Denver toward a busy intersection. He saw the light was green and the car in front of him signaled to turn right. Knowing that he would be able to cruise through the intersection, he took his eye off of the road for a second. The car in front of him halted abruptly to let a pedestrian cross the boulevard. Rex was too close; he couldn't stop in time. He smashed into the car going twenty miles an hour. He hit the rear window, and the velocity of the impact catapulted him over the roof, bouncing him off of the hood onto the street. He ended up laid out, stunned from the collision.

"Oh, dear God, what did I do? Are you hurt? I'm going to call the police," said the thirty-something driver in a panic as he jumped out of his car, scrambling to where Rex lay on the ground.

"No, I'm not hurt. I'm all right," said Rex, shaking it off, looking up at man wearing a tight pink Polo shirt standing over him.

"This is the worst day of my life. I have to call 911." The driver was aghast and crying hysterically after noticing that Rex was missing a leg.

"Sir, really, I'm OK. Just bring me my bike, and help me up."

"Oh, God! I ran over a one-legged man."

"Bring me my fucking bike, and help me up! Please."

Rex reassured the man several times that he was not hurt. The driver regained his wits enough to recover Rex's bicycle, which was badly bent, but still ridable, and helped him up. Rex sat on his bicycle, proving to the fellow that it wasn't necessary to go to the hospital. Still crying, the driver got in his car and drove away talking to himself.

The bike frame was bent in such a way that the front wheel would not turn to the right or the left. Each time Rex changed directions, he had to stop, step off, pick up the bike, and point the whole frame to face the direction he needed to go.

18

MEETING ANDY

Rex, now conditioned enough to bicycle a long distance, at the suggestion of some friends, signed up to ride in the local children's hospital fundraiser. In June 1991, he participated in The Courage Classic, a 225-mile ride over three days. He didn't know what to expect – he simply knew he loved to ride and carried a soft spot in his heart for kids.

During the dinner of Day One, a time of recognition was held for some of the participants. Dr. Andy Pruitt, director of the Boulder Sports Medicine Clinic, a below-the-knee amputee and two-time world disabled cycling champion, spoke about his involvement to raise awareness for the disabled community and spotlighted the group of teenage amputees he was overseeing. After dinner, many people went up to Dr. Pruitt to talk to him. Rex chose to not fight the crowd and made a mental note to find him the next day.

Under blue skies and billowy clouds, riding his old, borrowed clunker, Rex, sifted through the crowd of participants, searching for the handicapped group. When he rode up to them, the riders were positioned closely around Andy, listening as he taught his group of amputees to form a paceline and draft off of the rider in front of them. Rex joined in.

"Drafting is an energy-saving technique that takes advantage of the slipstream created by the front rider," said Andy. "The rider at the front of the line cuts through the wind, decreasing the resistance for the second cyclist who then does not have to work as hard. When several riders are participating, they line up one behind the other to form a paceline. It's understood that each will take a turn being the front rider. OK, let's go."

Rex had only ridden by himself until then and had not experienced the effect of drafting. He liked his first taste of sitting on another guy's wheel. While Andy led his group up the backside of Drake toward Devil's Gulch, his group dispersed. Rex stayed latched onto Andy's airstream.

"Rex, there's a pace car that will pick you up if you can't make it to the top of Devil's Gulch," said Andy, guessing that Rex must be tired from riding the clunker bike and that was why he stayed so close.

Rex looked up at the steep incline ahead of him, "I'll be all right," he said, then lowered his gear and pressed on, hoping his tires would hold out.

"OK, but it's there for us. We can't get off of our bike and walk up like the able-bodied people can. I'll see you up there." Andy broke away.

Rex pushed down and pulled up on the pedal of his old beater, passing people who quit and took the pace car. He pulled ahead of able-bodied riders, too, who midway up the mountain were exhausted and had to get off their bikes and walk to the top. Rex raised his head and saw Dr. Pruitt at the crest looking down at the group of riders. Refusing to opt for the car, Rex summoned every bit of physical and psychological power he possessed, determined to conquer the 18 percent grade.

The able-bodied riders walking their bikes cheered as Rex passed them. Even other riders were cheering him on as one by one he inched passed. Rex loved the positive attention and it motivated him to labor even harder. The burning in his thigh was excruciating and his biceps and triceps were on fire from pumping down and up on the handlebars with each pedal stroke, his upper body motion equivalent to that of a push-up.

Drenched in sweat and gasping for air, he rode up next to Andy, "I made it."

"Rex, I was studying the way you ride, pushing down and pulling up on the pedal. Most people only push down, and don't think to pull up as well. Your arms must be tired too, from all that pumping. I doubted that you would make it. I'm impressed," said Andy. "Look around, you're the only above-the-knee amputee to make it to the top, and on that bike. That's pretty unbelievable, Rex."

Rex, emotionally inflated from the accolade, stuck his chest out, proud of his accomplishment. Although, it was only in his mind's eye. He was too tired to sit up straight.

On the final day of the fundraiser, they rode one hundred miles along the Peak-to-Peak Highway, ending up at their starting point in Boulder.

"Have you ever thought about racing?" asked Andy, in the hotel parking lot, while packing up is gear.

"Is there a place for me to compete?"

"Well, Rex, I'm an amputee world champion. There is a venue for you and you should think about racing."

"There is? How do I get started?" asked Rex, beaming.

"You'll need to get better equipment and train regularly. I don't know how you made it through the ride on that rust bucket you've got there. Give me a call," said Andy, handing Rex his business card.

19

TRAINING

Rex opened the top right drawer to his desk at the community center and pulled out a business card to the Boulder Center for Sports Medicine. He tapped the card on the grey metal desk then dialed the number to Dr. Pruitt, whom he had met on the children's hospital fundraiser ride. "Andy, I thought about what you said, and I'd like to compete."

Andy told Rex he would have to work out five days and ride about 300 miles a week. That was the commitment required to be competitive.

Rex wasn't mentally prepared for that answer. His dream of cycling had grown since that day in the yard with Skeeter, however, the dream wasn't yet big enough to encompass all the work and sacrifice it would cost.

"Rex, it takes a lot of effort to win. My guess is, from watching you ride up Devil's Gulch, you want to win. Am I right?"

"Yeah, I want to win, but that's a lot of training. I have a job." Thoughts darted through Rex's mind about his new responsibilities at the Community Care Center and supporting himself financially.

"When people are passionate about something, Rex, they figure it out. Just start and see what happens. I believe you can do it. Call me in a week."

The prospect of preparing to become a competitor was daunting. Fortunately, there were parallels he could draw upon for invigoration and confidence. If he exhibited the inner resilience to do whatever it took to quit heroin and cigarettes, he toted the backbone for this as well. Even so, he was momentarily seized by his old mental default setting.

I don't belong to a gym. I can't afford to join one. I need a new bike, thought Rex, falling prey to the obstacles scattered along the path before him. With a sinking heart, he called on a buddy to help him see past the barriers.

"Hey man, it's Rex, my new coach laid out a training plan for me and I'm all twisted up over it." Rex explained that he didn't think he could do what Andy said was necessary. Plus, he couldn't afford a gym membership.

While listening to Rex's dilemma, Scott hatched a plan. "I'll pick you up at 5 a.m. tomorrow. Be ready."

"Uh, what's your plan?" asked Rex, a little skeptical.

"Just be ready."

The alarm sounded at 4:30 a.m. startling Rex. He wasn't used to waking up that early. In ten minutes he was ready, he sat by the door trying to stay awake. Jolted again by the sound of his friend honking the car horn, he went out into the dark morning.

"Here hold onto this," said Scott, handing Rex a jar of change.

"What's this for?"

"The gym!"

Scott explained that he worked at a hospital where the employees could use the workout room for free and a family member could join for a one-time fee of sixty dollars.

"We're going to pay with this jar of pennies?" asked Rex.

"Yeah, that should cover the cost. We'll tell them you're my significant other."

"OK, whatever you say. This should be interesting."

166

The walk into this hospital was completely different from his walk into the psychiatric hospital and down the hall of stench, all those years ago. He was full of optimism and excitement, even felt giddy about their plan. This time, he knew without a doubt that he was doing the right thing. They walked down a long fluorescent-lit corridor that smelled of freshly sprayed Glade. Strutting up to the counter in the gym, Scott authoritatively began talking to the cute girl at the front desk.

"This is Rex, my significant other and he wants to join the gym."

"Your significant other. So, you two are togeth…?"

"This should cover the fee," Scott cut her off before she could finish her sentence. "See ya, Rex." Scott rushed out the door.

"Wait, what do….?" Rex, bewildered, turned to the girl and smiled.

Feeling awkward, Rex hurried over to the weight lifting area to avoid any further questioning about what transpired and left the girl alone to count the change.

Rex sat down on the end of the bench, leaned down and picked up one twenty-pound dumbbell with his right hand. He rested his elbow on his thigh and began his first set of bicep curls. An overweight lady walking on the treadmill on the other side of the small area looked at him and smiled.

"Good morning. You too, huh?" she asked Rex, as she toweled off her neck.

"Yeah, me too," answered Rex, knowing exactly what she meant. That it was time to buckle down and get in shape. Who else goes to the gym at 5:00 a.m., besides the fiercely dedicated. Unlike snow skiing or cycling, working out in the gym was not fun, especially in the first days. There was no wind tousling his hair, no fresh air to breathe, no new sights to stumble upon, but every morning he got up and rode with Scott to the hospital.

On the fourth morning, Rex reached his arm out, aching from the previous day's workout, and pressed the button to turn the alarm off, the clock read 4:30. Immediately the old monkeys of negativity and self-destruction were lurking, ready to pounce. He shook his head as they tried to dominate his thinking while he was still groggy and defenseless, hoping to derail his progress. He pulled the covers over his head wanting nothing more than to pick up the phone and call his friend to tell him he wouldn't be going today, then curl up and cry. Instead, sweating from the heat of his breath in that confined space, he prayed. "God, I need some help here." As if an instant answer to his prayer, the phone rang. "On my way, be

168

there in ten minutes," said his friend. Rex worked out five days a week and did not deviate.

During this time he was also working on Step 4 of the Twelve Steps. "Take a searching and fearless moral inventory of ourselves." Rex scoured through his childhood and rooted out resentments he'd been carrying around for so long they developed into ferocious hatred.

He recalled how his dad enjoyed mowing the lawn on Saturday mornings. Lendy would fix a large plastic cup of iced tea, which he set on the wrought iron table on their front porch. He would drape an old ragged towel around his neck and push the mower back and forth across the lawn in neat rows, making sure the tires lined up precisely in the groove of the previous path.

Once, while his dad was priming the lawnmower in the front yard, Rex snuck into the garage and gathered up a handful of Buckshot. Scattering the pellets throughout the grass in the back yard, he hoped that as his dad mowed over them, they would explode and cause him injury. He hated that man and he was bent on revenge. Rex longed to hurt him the way he had been hurt.

As Rex was analyzing this memory, he came to identify that what he intended was not for his father to hurt physically. He wanted him to hurt emotionally, on the inside. However, as a young boy, his mental capacity to differentiate between the two was not developed. During this time of intense soul searching, Rex uncovered another person he hated with the same vehemence. That person was himself.

As he participated in this assignment, he examined the bad things he inflicted and the hurt he caused others. These memories were parasites loitering below the surface that needed to be eradicated. It was a cleansing from a life that he pledged never to relive.

As painful as it was, he stared down the wreckage of his past, knowing it was his path to freedom. Just as he trained to physical exhaustion every day, so did he faithfully write … until he was mentally depleted.

October 1991

I've put so many people through hell. At the time I could have cared less, I just wanted what I wanted and didn't give a shit about anything else. The time I fell asleep in the living room with a lit cigarette in my mouth and almost burned down the house in Tulsa, I didn't care. Even though the smoke ruined everything in the house. Ann was upset. I just thought about how I should get the insurance money, since I was the one that caused the fire. All of her family pictures were ruined. I'm an idiot.

All the times I stole money from my grandparents. After all, they did for me and Roger. I caused them so much heart-ache. No wonder they shipped us off to California. It's too late to tell them I'm sorry.

That bastard of a dad. I hate that son-of-a-bitch. It's his fault I'm the way I am. I don't know if I'll ever be able to see otherwise. He's fucking pathetic and so many times I wished he was dead or I plotted to kill him myself. This hate isn't doing me any good. I have to find a way to forgive that piece-of-shit. Just thinking that makes me want to puke. 'Where the fuck were you my whole life?' I'm a selfish bastard just like him.

OK, what's good about me. Anything? I have a good sense of humor. I can laugh at myself. I really do care about people. I want to help people. I work hard. I'm passionate and I'm a good friend. That wasn't as hard as I thought it would be.

171

Fearless about taking his inventory, Rex began to comprehend the scope to which the lies of his addiction deceived him. He learned his addiction caused him to surmise there was only bad in the world; that was all that he could see. With each new journal entry, he wiped away from his tear-filled eyes, a little more of the crust of deception. As the scab became smaller, the better traits within him and the world around him came into view.

Engrossed in the process of Step 4, he realized his animosity toward his dad blinded him to his father's good traits. He feverishly assessed and wrote about this area of his life, and observed in himself that his dad and he were the same, except that his dad never got to behold his own worth. Now mindful of the positive qualities about himself and cognizant that his dad embodied all of those same attributes, he sadly felt his dad had kept his light shrouded under the darkness of drugs and alcohol. *The only difference between us*, thought Rex, *was I sought recovery and he didn't.*

"Dad, I forgive you. Please forgive me," he uttered, prostrate and weeping.

When he was able to sit up, he knew a deep, monumental moment occurred. Rex let go of the vicious contempt he had been harboring toward his father and crossed a juncture of true healing. Set free from years of bondage propelled by pent up

172

bitterness, he fell prone again and finally mourned the loss of his father who, in 1988, died ravaged and friendless, on the grungy bathroom floor in an abandoned trailer.

No longer ashamed of who he was and where he came from, Rex yearned for someone to know him from top to bottom, from good to bad. He did not want to die forsaken and lonely the way his father did.

Restored to sanity, Rex watched his world replenish itself with the beauty and love that come from making healthy choices. Each success perpetuated another. This motivated him to keep pushing through no matter how crushing the inertia of old patterns bore down, or how fruitless his efforts seemed. While gaining control over his physical body, he continued to confront his internal demons, determined to conquer those as well. Far down in his bones, he knew victory was no longer just for other people. It was for him now, too, and he devoted all of his energy toward realizing it spiritually, physically, and mentally.

Rex diligently kept to the training routine Andy prescribed and two of Andy's friends, Marc and Brad, became his riding partners.

Many times it was just Rex and Marc. A routine would be prescribed for Rex, and Marc would ride along with him. "I

173

remember after The Courage Classic, Andy was excited about meeting you, Rex. Marc was making conversation while they unloaded bikes at their meet-up spot. "He said, I got this guy who made it up Devil's Gulch with one leg. Most riders with two legs can't do it."

"I wasn't sure I was going to make it up myself." Rex and Marc secured their water bottles in their holders and pedaled west out of Boulder.

The routines varied between endurance, climbing, accelerations and sprinting workouts, depending on what type of conditioning Rex needed to do. He and Marc would start early in the morning, ride for a few hours, ending the ride with lunch at Le Peep restaurant, in Boulder. Once in a while, though, the old Rex seeped through.

"Fuck!" yelled Rex as he and Marc were riding on the diagonal on Hover Road.

"What happened?" asked Marc.

"The stupid crank broke."

"Well, pull over so we can take a look at it," said Marc.

They were thirteen miles out from where their cars were parked at the Flatiron Athletic Club in Boulder. If the pedal broke on an able-bodied person's bike, they could still ride using only one side of the bike. Since Rex didn't use two pedals, he removed the left crank, rendering his bike unrideable if the right side broke.

"You go on man, I'm going to walk back," said Rex.

"Don't be ridiculous! Let's flag down a vehicle."

"I don't want a ride," said Rex, who didn't want to be perceived as weak.

"Rex, your bike broke. It happens," said Marc, flagging down an approaching vehicle.

Still learning to process his confusion of genuine help and concern from others as pity, he battled hard against the triggers that caused him to feel like less of a man because his body was not whole.

"Shit, I'll take the fucking ride. Just don't tell anyone."

"Rex, I won't. Your bike broke, you're just taking a ride back to town."

"I don't care, I don't want any help," said Rex, as he threw his bike into the back of the truck that stopped.

20

FIRST RACE

The living room curtains swayed in the fresh, cool October 1991 breeze, as Rex brewed a pot of tea. He felt rested after sleeping in late and foregoing his Sunday morning ride. His riding partner Brad, now one of his coaches, was trying to instill in Rex that training too much would end up hindering his progress, that it would keep him drained of enough energy to ride hard the last few laps of a race. Rex preferred training to rest, yet he knew he needed to listen to his coach. This was the perfect day to sit around and watch the Broncos game.

Skeeter hurled the pitted, red Nerf football across the living room to Rex, who was sitting up on the overstuffed, dingy recliner, pumping his fists in the air.

"That was awesome," said Skeeter.

"Come on Broncos, the game ain't over yet, you still have plenty of time for Elway to work some magic. Hey, can you get me a refill?"

"Sure thing," answered Skeeter, who was heading toward the kitchen. "I'll get it," he said when the phone rang. "It's for you." Skeeter handed Rex the phone and went to the kitchen. "What a fucking slaughter." Skeeter mumbled to himself.

"Hello."

"Rex, it's Andy. What a game, huh?

"Yeah, a sorry game."

"Hey, the reason I'm calling is, there's a race coming up that I think you should enter."

"I'm listening," answered Rex, nodding to Skeeter as he handed him his refilled tea.

"Yeah, it's a category four Circuit, 25 miles."

"So, you think I'm ready?"

"That's what we need to find out." Andy told Rex the race was an entry-level competition for able-bodied riders. Each lap was 12.5 miles. There are some long flats, and a couple of good hills. "It will give you a good idea of what racing is all about and where your skill level is compared to other athletes."

"When is it?" asked Rex, excited and nervous to apply his training in a real situation.

"It's next Sunday for Columbus Day weekend."

Rex hung up the phone and sat in shock, his mouth wide open.

"What was that?" asked Skeeter.

"I'm going to race next weekend."

"Hell yeah! Just do better than the Broncos did today."

Preparing for his upcoming race, Rex rode his weekly 350 miles more focused than ever. On race day, he left early giving himself plenty of time. He wanted to use the drive to relax his body. It didn't work. He was too wound up.

Filled with uncertainty, Rex followed the signs to the parking lot for the event. He slowed at the handicap stalls, but decided to bypass them and parked at the end of the row instead. Andy warned him that he would be judged by his appearance. Showing any signs of vulnerability, like parking in the handicap spot, would increase the competitor's perception of weakness in him. As much as he could, he wanted to appear strong and in control.

"Can I help you?" asked a race official, who noticed Rex looking out of place, rolling his bike then hopping up to it, rolling and hopping, rolling and hopping.

"Uh, yeah. Where do I go to register?" Rex's wish of appearing like a pro, dashed.

"You're entering the race?"

"Yeah."

"It's over there. Keep walking that way and you will run into the sign-up table," the official said, his arm stretched out pointing to the right.

"Thanks. Oh, hey, what do I do with my bike?"

"Just keep it with you. Good luck, today."

While making his way toward the registration table, Rex was struck with a rude reality check. The other racers, dressed in top-of-the-line bike shorts and coordinated Trek jerseys, were wiping down their Carrera bikes that resembled rocket ships. Cycling apparel and high-tech bikes were just a wish for him. He was wearing a pair of lycra shorts from a discount store and still riding a loaner bike that looked like it was made out of strung-together beer cans, with a clunky gear shift. It did not measure up next to the sleek lines and shiny chrome of his competitors' bikes. In a sport where status matters, he touted none.

179

Over the loudspeaker, the announcer called for the competitors to make their way to the start line. Rex, the only one-legged rider, fell in with the 120 cyclists, who seemed eager to hear the gun go off. Intimidated, Rex looked around at the sea of bikes. They were packed in tight, too tight. He glanced down at the pedal on the bike next to him, one foot away and wondered, *What if I get knocked over? Will I get trampled by a bunch of bicycles? Would that cause a big pile up? What the hell am I doing?*

The energy of the crowd intensified, when the speaker announced, "one minute to start." Rex's senses heightened and the smells around him became overpowering. The coconut sunscreen lotion lingering to the right and menthol wafting from the left, made it hard to breathe. The myriad of sounds, coughing, spitting, chatter, his foot tapping the pavement, became deafening and he was lost in a blur of sensory overload.

Like claustrophobia, the surroundings closed in on him, and he didn't hear the announcer call out ten-seconds. The crowd collectively stiffened, which grabbed his attention and alerted to him that something important was happening. The announcer call eight-seconds, seven, six, five, silence. *What the hell? Did they stop the race?* Confused, Rex didn't know the counting stopped at five-seconds.

"Oh shit, here we go," he said aloud, as the gun blasted and the crowd started to move as one large unit, like a flock of birds migrating.

He centered his butt on the saddle and slid his foot into the pedal strap. It only took a second; he practiced that move one thousand times by then, making it second nature. He ratcheted his pedal over and over, halfway up then down as fast as he could, to pick up speed. Panting from the anxiety of the start line and soggy from the sweat pouring down the back of his neck, he felt submerged in a roar of buzzing tires. *Just keep pedaling, you've been through worse. You can do this, breathe. Slow deep breaths, in through the nose out through the mouth, slow and steady.*

About three miles into the race, he dared to look up from the tire whizzing in front of his wheel. The cyclists had spread out a little. He was surprised and relieved that there was more space between riders than he expected. The wind in his face was refreshing and gave him a burst of energy. He looked behind him and discovered he was right around the middle of the paceline.

Approaching the first hill, he was confident he would gain standing because he was strong on the inclines. He pedaled harder, wanting to gain momentum and make headway by the time he reached the top of the hill, but unknowingly was expending too much energy that early in the race. He didn't yet know how to pace his strength and was still learning strategy and bike handling skills.

He managed to stay in the middle for the first lap of the race even though he was having trouble holding the line, a sure sign to the other riders he was on the ropes. Two miles into the second lap his reserves reached dangerously low and one by one the cyclists in the rear passed him. At the fifth mile, Rex looked back and saw a long lonely stretch of highway. His heart sank as he kept pulling up and pushing down on his pedal. Even aware of his imminent failure, he completed what he started and crossed the finish line dead last.

Not caring about who came in first, the ceremony afterward, or what his official time was, he rode his bike straight to his truck, and left the event. During the hour-long drive home, a loud interior voice rose up and reminded him he was nobody. *Who are you to think you could compete and be good at this?* He was embarrassed about his performance; and his self-centeredness, which couldn't stand to be humiliated, got the best of him. Reluctantly, when he got home, he called Andy and told him he came in dead last.

"I worked as hard as I could for half the race, then my leg gave out. I don't know what I was thinking."

"What do you mean? Are you telling me you want to quit, already?"

"Yeah."

"Rex, you stayed with the group of able-bodied young guys for a lot of the race and got dropped before the end, so what?"

"So what? I came in last! I was the very last person to cross the finish line."

"Rex, we all got dropped in our first race. It's not a big deal."

"I guess, I just thought, I was better than I really am."

"It was your first race. Why don't you readjust your expectations and try again?"

After talking to Andy, Rex was able to appreciate what he pulled off. He'd stayed up with younger two-legged cyclists almost the whole time, and it was an accomplishment to be proud of.

Rex entered more competitions. Longer Road Races, Circuits, and Criteriums. Some went well, some were frustrating. Others were downright miserable. Even so, he was more determined than ever to become a contender.

Saturday 7 a.m. group rides were a staple in Rex's training. He would join Andy, Marc, Brad and whoever else showed at the meet-up site in Boulder to hone their skills. One such morning while on the Peak to Peak highway, the paceline of riders was moving at 35 miles per hour on the flat. Rex was fifth from the front. He felt weak in his ability to attack and his trainer agreed that he needed development in that area.

Rex saw the front rider, in his training group, tap his elbow signaling to the second man that he was going to move from the front of the pack to the back. Rex, now better at strategy waited to strike. He passed the rider and heard the last guy in the paceline say to the rider, "get on." That lets the rider transitioning to the end know who the last person is and that it is safe to rejoin the paceline. It was then that Rex made his move. It was harder to detect Rex breaking away because he couldn't stand up, normally an alert to other riders that someone was breaking away. He threw his gear, moved out and pushed his pedal down as hard as he could.

When he pulled up on his pedal the strap broke, and his foot flew off. It forced his unbalanced body down hard to the right, causing him to skid and tumble across 10 feet of pavement. Shaken and covered in large splotches of strawberry red road rash, he sat trying to regain the breath that had been knocked out of him.

"Rex, you OK?" asked Brad, hurrying over.

"I think so. I just need a minute," Rex said, dazed.

"Take all the time you need. I'll ride back with you." Brad sat down and brushed the asphalt from Rex's body.

"No, man. You guys keep going."

"It's all right. You guys go on," Brad said to the other riders. "I'll stay. He's hurt pretty bad."

"I'll be fine. You go on. Just bring my bike over here."

With help from his training partners, and choosing to use that wipe-out as even more motivation, Rex honed his skills. His perseverance paid off, and he started winning. By March, Rex qualified to compete in the Disabled National Championships in the summer of 1992.

Along with the wins, he also attributed his success to realizing that everything didn't have to end up with the outcome he deemed it should. When he lay down at the end of the day, and examined his life, he understood that it was his part to get up every day, train, stay clean, and make choices that would spur him ahead.

One night just before he closed his eyes, he acknowledged the force outside of himself, guiding his new life, and like a toddler learning to walk, knew he was not in control of it. Subsequent to the profuse and challenging internal work of Steps 3 (Made a decision to turn our will and our lives over to the care of God as we understood God) and 4, (Made a searching and fearless moral inventory of ourselves) he concluded that it was necessary for him to surrender to that force and he, at last, turned his will and his life over to God, as he understood Him; someone who was on his side.

Empowered by this realization and fueled by his passion for riding, when Rex dug down within himself he found a new storehouse of vigor previously unknown to him. By yielding to God's guidance, he also reached an expanse of spirituality he did not know existed and tuned in to the supernatural realm, where miracles occur.

His body drained and heavy from all the physical exercise, Rex pulled himself up in the early mornings, much like he did when he first began going to the hospital gym. It was a little easier to rise before dawn, now that the bitter cold of winter had passed, however, Rex was no less exhausted. Yawning, he made his way to the kitchen where he filled his Denver Bronco's mug to the brim with piping hot coffee. He blew on the Columbian roast before taking a sip, then set the mug down on the counter next to the sink. In the mornings he nourished himself with a glass of freshly made juice. It was Wednesday, the day he made a new batch. Carrots, beets, celery and spinach still wet from being rinsed, lined the tile counter. One by one he stuffed the vegetables into the Jack

Lalanne Juicer, making sure the cup to catch the juice stayed centered under the faucet. He filled his pitcher with the orange liquid and poured the rest into a glass to drink. It was better cold, but the first glass of a new batch was always room temperature. He downed it in two big swallows. He rinsed out the machine, topped off his coffee and sat down at the table to pray.

Admonished as a boy not to pray for himself or what he wished for, his morning prayer went like this: "God, if what I am doing is going to help people, I will do the work and the results are up to you. If what I'm doing is going to be of service, I'll work as hard as I can work, although I'm tired and I don't know what to do." The prayer lifted his spirit, but not his physical body.

From where Rex was sitting, he could see the temperature dial. It read 46 degrees this mid-spring morning. The snow melted and slate skies gave way to welcomed sunshine. Still, he had to drag himself onto his bike feeling unable to reach the end of the block. It was like that for weeks, yet it never failed – when he crossed ten miles down the parkway, suddenly he felt like he could ride forever.

21

DISABLED NATIONAL CHAMPIONSHIPS

As Rex began to show more and more promise of having the moxie to win, he began working with a coach. Brad, who accompanied Rex on training rides, helped him with technique and strategy, officially became his Colorado coach. The two spent hours talking about racing: knowing when to attack, when to hold back and the importance of resting. Brad worked hard to get Rex prepared for his next big race and now it was time to see if it would pay off.

Rex arrived at the Disabled National Championships in June 1992, schlepping his new three hundred dollar bike with the left crank removed. It wasn't a rocket ship, but it was a big step up from the clunker he had been riding. Another life metaphor, of how far he'd come and the distance still to go. It was his only bike.

When he looked around and saw that the other racers had personal mechanics fine-tuning their bikes custom made for each specific race, he was unaffected. He was there to contend. He closed his eyes, lifted his prayer and went out to loosen up. His yellow and white off-brand cycling shirt fit taught around his now ripped upper body. Sitting on the ground with his leg out straight, the jersey colors expanded each time he stretched out to touch his toes, his belly no longer prohibiting him to bend forward. He retrieved his sunscreen from the back zippered pocket on his jersey and applied it generously to his arms and face, except not above his eyes. He found out the hard way to avoid that area when sunscreen-filled sweat dripped into his eyes causing them to sting and water, making it hard to see. Smelling of Pina Colada, he was ready to race.

The first of three contests were Time Trials in which a rider competes alone against the clock. An individual Time Trial race is referred to as "the race of truth." The racer relies only on his own strength and endurance. He cannot take advantage of teammates or the slipstream from a pack. The rider with the fastest time is the winner. For this type of race, special aerodynamic bikes are used with handlebars that sit lower on the bike allowing the rider to rest their elbows on a pad, like an armrest, and position their forearms in line with the wind. This causes the rider's back to sit as low and flat as possible, which distributes the airflow around the body. Rex didn't even have Time Trial handlebars.

Knowing he was going to have to work harder than ever, he didn't dwell on the unfair advantage of his competitors and went to the start line, of which he was now familiar. The familiar and rhythmic pounding of his heart joined him as it always did. He learned to harness the adrenalin rush and used it to keep him alert and focused while the announcer counted down. Coach Brad gave last words of advice while holding Rex's bike steady at the start line. "Keep your back flat and pedal your ass off. You've got this." The gunshot sounded, Coach Brad let go and Rex bolted around the track with one thing on his mind; the upcoming Paralympics. Hunched down to discomfort, he made his body as small and flat as possible. After the second lap, pain began to sear through his lower back, which was not conditioned for that form. Keeping his back low and flat caused his neck to spasm due to holding his head up in an unnatural position. His fingers clamped tight around the handlebars as he whizzed around the track, scoring a second place. The first place winner beat him by a fraction of a second.

Believing he gave everything he could muster, he was satisfied with that placement. This was his first true match up to other disabled contenders and he was happy knowing his skill level was right there with the best.

The following day was his favorite kind of event, a Criterium. Crits are fast, intense, dangerous. It's not the best rider that wins, it's the strongest fighter. The guy with the win-at-all-cost mentality who will play a little dirty if he has to. There is no room for fear in a high-level Criterium. The racers afraid to crash come in last. Like a chess game, you have to think three moves ahead and consider what moves your opponents are going to make. Strategy is as important as strength.

The race was set up on a one-mile-loop barricaded off through the city streets. The track included four corners; two turned right and two turned left. It was 40 minutes long plus two laps.

Brad met Rex on the patch of grass near the registration table where riders gathered to stretch. "Rex, I want you to sit in the middle of the front ten for a while. Find out who the strong guys are, and position yourself with them, however, don't take the lead." Rex listened to his pre-race pep talk. "Don't be afraid to sit-in for a while and conserve your energy, be patient." Rex rolled onto his back and placed his calf on Brad's shoulder. Brad leaned forward, stretching Rex's hamstrings and glutes. "They're going to be watching you too, especially after yesterday."

"I'm ready. Let's win this one!"

Rex rolled up to the start line unfazed by the sea of bicycles around him. He sat with his butt half off of the seat enabling him to stand up on his right leg. The horn sounded he gave two quick pushes from his right foot, clicked his cleat into the pedal as it was going down, centered himself on the seat and began his ratcheting motion; pulling up on the pedal halfway, pushing down, pulling up halfway, pushing down.

Established with the front ten riders within the first few laps, Rex noticed one of them was the current national champion. He felt a sense of belonging wash over him; it was odd and he didn't know what it was, but didn't dismiss it. He let his emotion take its course while he was sitting in at the back of the group and realized for the first time it was natural for him to believe he belonged with the winners. He heeded his coaches advise to conserve his energy and stayed with that group content in the inner healing he just experienced of truly being worthy to win.

Rex had advantages and disadvantages to banking the corners. Since his center of gravity was altered, he didn't carry an even weight distribution across his bike. Because of this, turning right could be problematic. Turning left, though, was a benefit due to the removal of the crank on that side. That made it possible for him to lean way over and still pedal through using the right side.

The hair stood up on his arms when the pack compressed tightly, racing through the hairpin curves. He kept a close eye on the tires that sped all around him being alert of near misses and any openings that might come about,

Impatient, after a several laps, Rex no longer wanted to hold back. Positioned at the outside of the peloton, he blew through the first left bend at full speed, broke away, and attacked to the front of the group, and like the Time Trials, the only thing on his mind was the upcoming Paralympics. Now, accustomed to the roar of spinning tires, he sped through the pack and caught up to the current national champion, who yelled over to his teammates, "Let him go, he's not that good." Pedaling as hard as he could, drenched in sweat, and transfixed on his front tire,

Rex lapped the whole peloton. Still anxious he wasn't going to win, he prayed hard, "God, if this is what is right, then, God, you keep me going, you keep me going."

Rex went to the front of the pack again. This time the national champion rode up alongside him and counseled, "slow down, you're going to be all right."

Rex understood what he meant, that he didn't need to work so hard, he was going to win, after all, he lapped the entire group of riders. Rex backed off, the burning in his thigh subsided.

He won the second contest by minutes.

The third and final stage was a Circuit race, Rex scored another second place. His high ranking qualified him to compete in the Paralympic Games in Barcelona, in September of 1992.

Two days later, at his Tuesday night meeting, elated, Rex told his fellowship and friends he secured a position on the Paralympic cycling team. Listening open-mouthed as Rex chronicled his achievement, the proud and thrilled group, who had slowly become his family, decided to organize fundraisers to help Rex with the cost of the trip. The Paralympics did not pay for travel expenses.

Over the next few months, his chosen family held barbecues at their homes and collected special donations. Little by little, friends and strangers pitched in until there was enough for a round trip ticket to Spain and some spending money.

The day before his departure to Barcelona, the dark grey clouds subdued the sunlight as Rex placed the last T-shirt in his suitcase and safely stowed his bicycle in its traveling container. The rain pelted against the kitchen window near where he set his plane ticket and passport on the counter so he wouldn't forget them early in the morning. As he stared out the water-blurred glass, he mentally went over his checklist one more time. *Gloves, cleats, camera, sunscreen, address book, aspirin, cough drops.*

Rex was as ready as he'd ever been to board the airplane that would fly him across the ocean to the most exciting time of his newly sober life. But first, an evening out, a send-off party with the people who made it possible for him to go. When his good friend, Bobby, pulled up in the driveway, Rex was out the front door before Bobby turned off the car engine. The rain had slowed to a drizzle, leaving only droplets of water on Rex's ponytail that hung below his baseball cap.

The closer they drove to the amphitheater, the harder the rain was falling, again, though it wasn't a worry. Due to the stage's ample covering, concerts weren't canceled because of rain. "I thought the weather would make some people change their minds, but everybody is still coming," said Bobby, turning the windshield wipers to a faster speed.

"Good! I'm all packed and ready for tomorrow morning. So tonight, let's go have some fun."

Rex and his group of friends sang, danced, and laughed through the whole show, sober and free from the constraints of addiction.

On the ride home, Bobby reiterated how proud he was of Rex and what an inspiration he was to so many people. "You didn't think you could just slip out and nobody notice, did you?"

"No, I knew better. I just appreciate all you've done. It's good to have real friends." As he sat in the passenger seat listening to the rain, fear, curiosity, and gratitude cascaded over him.

The morning after the concert, Rex's body ached and his head felt heavy. When he sat up nausea welled to his throat demanding he lay back down. He shifted a bit before finding a comfortable position on his side. The small square black clock on his nightstand read 7:10, he stared at it and gave himself five more minutes. Bobby would be there at 7:40 to drive him to the airport.

The five minutes went in a flash. With no more time to waste. Rex sucked it up, showered off and managed to keep down a handful of vitamins. He looked forward to being on the plane where he could sleep during the four-hour flight from Denver to New York, where he would catch his connection to Spain.

22

GOING TO BARCELONA

Rex woke from deep sleep to the bumping and jolting of the airplane landing at JFK. The velocity pushed him forward as the plane roared down the runway before slowing to a taxi. Still groggy from his extended nap, he disembarked, and as he walked the long corridor toward his next terminal, he noticed the airport history timeline hanging on the walls in large black and white photographs.

The first was a print of Idylwild Golf Course, which was on that land before the airport, and from which the airport derived its original name. Another picture featured President Harry Truman attending the opening ceremony of the newly named New York International Airport, Anderson Field. After that, Rex bored with the history, sought out the nearest beverage stand and bought a cup of coffee. He dropped his seventy-nine cents into his fanny pack and knowing he had plenty of time, he sat and people-watched while he drank his fresh brew and inhaled the rising steam to loosen his congestion.

He watched a young exasperated mother walk by, loaded down with shoulder bags, doing her best to keep her toddler triplets close to her. Memories of playing with his niece and nephew in their room flooded his thoughts as he watched the children, all dressed in yellow striped shirts and blue jeans, clumsily run around their mother. A middle-aged man, hurried along in his navy blue suit. His right foot only lightly striking the floor as if there were a pebble in his shiny black loafer.

Part of Rex wanted to enthusiastically declare to the travelers passing by: *guess what, I'm going to the Paralympics in Barcelona, Spain. Me, an ex-drug addict, with one leg. Can you believe it? Me neither. It's true, it's fucking true!*

Emotions surged and swirled throughout his brain and body like the white foam of waves crashing against rocks as he followed the signs to International Departures. Just as he was able to put a name to one feeling, another came and sloshed it to-and-fro. He was flooded with excitement and uncertainty,

199

fear and courage. His first time going out of the country was to participate in one of the biggest sporting events in the world. As much as he loved competing on the ski slopes, this rush was unparalleled.

Dressed in his signature outfit of blue jeans with the left leg pinned up, tie-dyed shirt, Teva sandal, a baseball cap that covered his receding hairline, and ponytail that hung below his shoulders, he walked up to the crowded gate looking more like a hippy than an athlete. His 5' 10" inch frame had developed into a lean and muscular form, although it was hidden under his loosely fitting clothes, as was his still somewhat chubby middle section. His taut face, brown from the summer sun, made his slender nose appear longer, the downward slant more pronounced, and his brown eyes drooped on the outside corners. Together, it created an illusion that the upper part of his face was being pulled down, until it met with his square jaw and megawatt smile, to lift it back up.

He figured it would be clear to the other team members that the guy walking up to the departure gate on crutches with one leg was part of the Paralympics. However, he did not recognize the others as quickly, their disabilities were not as obvious as his. They were wearing prosthetics.

A slender man, about Rex's height, with olive skin and thick black hair, large black-framed glasses that covered over his cheekbones and a hint of a mustache, introduced himself. "Hey man, you must be Rex." Jose Alcala, the Paralympic coach for the amputee riders, extended his hand.

"Good to meet you," responded Rex, tucking his crutch in his armpit and reaching out to shake hands with Jose.

The team was comprised of competitors with below-the-knee amputations, above-the-knee amputations, missing upper limbs, cerebral palsy, and blind riders accompanied by their sighted partners, with whom they rode tandem, and three coaches.

Rex sat down between Erika and Corey two of the Cerebral Palsey contestants. Sitting in the seat straight across was Pier Beltrami, an Italian man, who was also an above-the-knee amputee. "I guess you're my competition." Rex joked, as he noticed Pier's pants pulled tight around the top of his prosthetic.

Just as Rex finished introducing himself to the people he would be living with for the next two weeks, it was time for the U.S. Paralympic team to board the airplane. Rex, along with the team, proudly made his way to the boarding entrance.

"Good luck to you," said a man who was closing up his computer.

"Go USA," said another man pumping his fist in the air.

"Make us proud," said a teenage girl, who was holding her little brother's hand.

Upon settling into his seat next to the window, Rex pointed the tiny overhead fan onto his face and closed his eyes. His heavy lids overrode the electricity in his belly and the sounds around him faded as he drifted off to sleep. Five hours into the eight-hour flight, he opened his eyes to find Jose, who was sitting next to him, reading a mystery novel. Rex re-wadded up his sweatshirt placed it on his shoulder to make a pillow and went back to sleep. When they landed in Barcelona the team gathered outside the arrival gate.

"Listen up, everyone. Let's make sure to stay together as we're making our way to customs," directed competitive cyclist and head coach Peter Paulding, a police chief from Pensacola Florida. "Make sure you have your passports and paperwork in a place easy to get to."

The cluster slowly navigated their way through bathroom stops and drink stands until they reached the long lines at the customs check-out. Travel weary from the time change and being cooped up on the plane for so long, Rex was becoming impatient, but used his better judgment and kept it to himself, not wanting to cause more problems. He overheard Peter ask an official if he could gather the individuals' information and check everyone through himself. The official said that wouldn't be possible. So the team waited in line for an hour and used up an additional hour to process through, then waited another hour for the shuttle to transport them to the Olympic Village.

Gray, rust, and dirt-colored geometric-patterned bricks paved the ground of the sprawling Olympic Village. Made of a metal mesh material, a sculpture of an enormous abstract whale with its tail curved up, glimmered bronze in the sunlight and appeared to hover above the square like an alien spaceship, overwhelming the area. The towering gray, metal cauldron that looked like a giant clip-art-whale diving down, was mounted to the side of the brick stadium. The massive flame, shooting out of the top, glowed in the sky, as an ever-present reminder of its symbology, "the struggle to victory."

In all of its grandeur, the Olympic Village was for Rex a distant second to the nature that surrounded him. He breathed in the warm salty air while he gazed at the palm tree-lined sidewalks set against the light and dark blue backdrop of the Mediterranean Sea and was revived after the seemingly endless travel.

The high-rise apartments were furnished with black, clean-lined furniture in the living quarters and provided space enough for roommates to move about comfortably.

The next day, September 3, 1992, Coach Jose, who shared an apartment with Rex and Pier, began to unpack and organize the teams gear stored in his living quarters.

"Anything I can help you with?" asked Rex.

"Yeah, help me sort this stuff out."

Rex sat on the floor and began categorizing cranks, chains, and tires while Jose assembled the bicycles.

The two men proceeded in their tasks and talked. Rex shared how he was a competitive snow skier in Colorado and needed something to do in the off season to stay in shape and his roommate had a bike. That was how he got involved in cycling only two years prior.

Jose began pulling the pieces out of another box."Rex, is this your bike, with one pedal?"

"Yeah, why?" Rex was neatly organizing his area along one of the living room walls.

"You only removed the crank arm and pedal?" Jose spread the parts out on the floor, and began to assemble Rex's bike.

"Yeah, that's it. I don't want to do anything that might give me an unfair advantage. That's not how I want to win." Rex straightened out the pile of chains.

"That's cool, man. I've seen just about everything out there, although I must say, I'm curious to see you ride." Jose flipped the bike up onto its wheels and leaned it against a chair. "At this point, I can't wrap my brain around you and a bicycle."

"Yeah, I thought my roommate lost his mind. It wasn't like I just picked up from the last time I rode a bike."

"So, you, in fact, did forget how to ride a bike. I thought that wasn't possible?" joked Jose, flinching, after Rex faked like he was going to throw a chain at him.

"Funny! Hey man, I'm going to get some rest and take care of this head cold."

Walking down the hall, Rex noticed Pier in the Bathroom combing his hair. "What are you doing?"

"Getting ready for the opening ceremony. Coach Peter told us to meet out front so we can all walk into the stadium together. Aren't you going?"

"No, man. I'm still fighting this cold." Rex headed down the hall toward his room. "I'd rather be healthy for the race."

"Wow, OK. Do what you have to do."

When Rex rose an hour later, the dorm was quiet. Thinking he was the only one there, he grabbed his crutches and went to the kitchen to get something to drink. As he reached the end of the hall, he startled Jose, still there sorting his inventory.

"Rex, you're still here? Why aren't you at the opening ceremony with everyone else?"

"I didn't want to go," said Rex, standing there in his underwear.

"Why not? It's a big deal." Jose stopped sorting equipment.

Rex thought about why he didn't want to go and answered. "It's just gimps on parade. I'm not going to be part of that spectacle."

To Rex, being a part of 'that spectacle' was declaring you wanted a sympathy vote. Like the people in the parade were celebrated more for being physically damaged in some way than they were for being athletes.

"Dude, that is so cruel. Lighten up." Jose was shocked by what Rex said.

"I'm here to race, not be giddy about the fact that half of my left side is missing."

"Suit yourself."

"Fuck it. I'm going to get something to drink," said Rex, as he heard the thunderous applause reverberating from the nearby stadium.

"Hey, you're in Limb Class 3, LC3, category because you're, AK, above-the-knee, right?" Jose went back to his task of organizing.

"Yep. How come you didn't go to the ceremony?" asked Rex, walking into the kitchen.

"I still had a lot to do, to be ready for tomorrow's race."

Rex gulped a glass of lukewarm Gatorade and sat down in the living room, now jam-packed with red, green, blue and yellow assembled bicycles and all the parts neatly categorized for the next day's race. He thumbed through the Paralympics pamphlet set on the glass-top end table beside the chrome-framed, black easy chair.

Highlights about the Olympic Village, the revitalizing of Barcelona and event information filled the pages. Three thousand athletes representing five continents were going to compete. Sixty-five thousand spectators were expected to be in attendance cheering for their country's men and women.

Before tossing the brochure back onto the table, he turned again to the front page where it read: "Sports Without Limits." Unaffected the first time he glanced at those words, this time he considered them.

"Hey, Jose, what do you think about this slogan?" Rex showed Jose the pamphlet.

"Yeah, I saw that. I don't know, maybe they're trying to get people to see what's possible. Like you can do more than you think you can."

Rex sat with that idea and realized his false pride slipped back in and attacked the part of him that still fell prey to the stigma of being disabled. The lying inner voice told him if he went with the others to the ceremony it would mean he was a gimp too. His protective mechanism caused him to judge the disabled community too harshly and that's why he didn't want to be identified with it on a world stage. He couldn't make sense of what he was feeling because he had competed in disabled sports for a couple of years and never reacted that way.

With pursed lips, he tapped the paper against his mouth and figured out that he was blindsided by his old destructive tapes and it deprived him of experiencing the open ceremony at his very first Paralympics. Resting his head on the back of the chair, he closed his eyes and concentrated on his breathing while fighting a silent battle in his mind. *I am a Paralympian. I deserve to be here. I can do whatever I put my mind to. God, if this is going to be of service to other people, then I will do the work.*

23

TRAINING IN BARCELONA

On a noncompeting day, Jose, coach of the LC3 group, who was also a Category 1 coach with the U.S. Cycling Federation and designer of conditioning regimens for able-bodied athletes, wanted to find out who displayed the best bike handling skills, prowess in knowing how to read a race, and strategic savviness, so Rex and the team gathered their bikes and met the coaches outside. Cumulus clouds filled the sapphire sky like gigantic pillars of whipped cream. Rex, as he had done many times by now, filled his lungs with the salty air and basked in the fair mid-seventies temperature, a wave of gratitude washed over him.

The wide walkways in the village doubled as training courses for bike handling and balance workouts. The team members lined up side by side, their red, blue, green and purple bikes and shirts formed a rainbow as they watched and one by one weaved through the homemade track.

As Pier took his turn, Rex observed where Pier's shoulders were in relation to his hips and how far he leaned opposite with his torso to counter-balance the weight of his hips. Drawing upon his mental notes from Pier's run, Rex zig zagged in and out of the orange pylons, forcing himself to lean farther and to shift his hips across the seat faster. He paid attention to the imbalance of his pelvis and how far he could transfer his weight from side to side before losing control and having to slow down.

Coach Jose pushed up on the rim of his large black-framed glasses that slid down his nose and studied Rex as he attacked the course. "Come on Rex, push yourself." Jose could already tell Rex was a strong rider.

"Hey man, just another day in paradise," said Rex, parking next to Pier, invigorated by the drill he just ran.

"There's no place I'd rather be right now," chimed Pier, raising his arms.

"I'm with you on that." Rex noticed Jose put a water bottle on the ground. "What's Jose got up his sleeve now?" Pier looked over.

"Hey, guys, listen up. Good job with the cones, now I want you to pick up some speed and when you pass by the water bottle, bend down and grab it and put it into your holder," instructed Jose. "OK, line up down at the cone."

"This ought to be fun," commented Pier.

"I'm going to have to think about this one," said Rex.

With high noon approaching, beads of sweat began to form on Rex's neck while he watched his teammates. When it was his turn, Rex went swiftly across the sidewalk, his eyes on the plastic bottle. "Come on, Rex. You got this," encouraged Pier.

Rex strategized during his approach: *if I lean to the left, I might fall and hit the concrete because I can't put a foot down to catch myself. If I lean to the right, I could fall over, the weight of my leg pulling me down.* He decided to use the left side and not lean as much, but instead bend down as far as he could using the strength of his core to keep him steady, stretching his arm down through the open space on that left side. By the third pass, he reached down far enough to pick up the water bottle without slowing down. "Good Job, Rex," the whole team said almost in unison.

211

On another off day, Jose drove his team into the Catalonia Mountains to the Montserrat Mountain Range, near Barcelona. This time he wanted to see who could keep tempo riding together, who could climb and ultimately who would emerge as the strongest riders.

The group feasted on the vast views of mystical fog-patches swirling through the valleys between the jagged peaks of the mountain range, as they pedaled their way to the four thousand foot elevation, Montserrat Monastery. The palatial buildings fleshy earth-tones blended with the cylindrical rocks of the mountainside jutting like rockets ready for takeoff. Forests of green oak trees added contrast to the barren mountains and gave off a woodsy aroma

Jose, riding in the team van, could see Rex's determination and skill at climbing. Rex was one of the first to make it up the incline. Being inspired by Rex's strength of character and fitness level, Jose began to seriously think about becoming more involved with disabled cycling and get them worked into a structure through the United States Cycling Federation, and the National Governing Body of competitive cycling. Jose wanted to integrate the disabled athletes into able-bodied sports organizations anticipating that they would become more visible.

Disabled cycling was still an emerging sport and therefore only had a few AK racers. Out of the two weeks Rex was at the Paralympics, his Limb Class 3 classification competed only one time.

The morning of his race, Rex began his internal dialogue early, telling himself: *think of it like any other race, find openings to make a move, don't try and do too much too fast, I'm a champion, that's why I'm here.* He carried on his silent mantra, pumping himself up and getting his mind focused for the biggest race of his short year-and-a-half competitive cycling career.

Rex pulled the bright red team jersey over his head and admired it in the mirror. He traced the white USA insignia placed across his heart with his forefinger and tugged on the white short sleeves, fitting snug around his biceps, embellished with a dark blue band circling the end. A blue triangle capped his shoulder area and he ran his palms down the large white stripe on the sides of the jersey. *This is really happening. How did I get here?*

Like a near-death experience, his past flashed through his mind. The fights with his dad, dishonorably discharged from the Navy, Triangle Park, all those rehab centers, the accident. It dawned on him at that moment: if he had not been in the accident, he would not be in Barcelona, Spain, competing in the 1992 Paralympics. He probably wouldn't even be riding a bike. He stopped himself there unwilling to let his thoughts travel further down the mind-path to the unthinkable.

For the first time, he entertained being thankful for the accident and the amputation of his left leg. He wasn't ready to go all the way and embrace it as a positive, but he allowed himself to peek into the possibility of this new conclusion.

Just a week before, he did not want to be identified as a "gimp." Now, maybe being a "gimp" saved his life. It was too much emotion to process before his race, so he shook it out of his head and returned to his self-talk. *I'm one of the best, I deserve this, I'm strong, I can win, I'm going to win.*

He gathered his red and black gloves, blue helmet and goggles and placed them near his reddish-brown bike. He secured a plastic water bottle into one of the holders on the inside of his bike frame. Other than the missing left pedal, his bicycle looked like any ten speed sold at a department store.

Rex, Pier, and Jose disembarked the Paralympic shuttle in Vall d'Hebron outside of Barcelona, where spectators were gathering to watch the race. At the start-line, Rex maintained his ritual of bowing his head and praying. "God, if this is going to be of service, I will do the work," he said, being mindful not to lose his attitude of service, especially at this momentous event where the stakes were high.

"Ten-seconds," called the announcer. Rex gripped the handlebars tighter while keeping his breath at a steady cadence. He knew now that breath control was just as important an element to victory as was strength, speed, and strategy.

The gun sounded and Rex pushed off with his right foot, clipped into the pedal and began his ratcheting motion. *This is just like any other race, this is the same as any other race. Who the fuck am I kidding? I'm representing my country here.* With that, Rex bolted to the front of the pack.

24

BARCELONA RACE

Rex stayed with the pack that emerged as the front riders. He noticed that out of the nine in the peloton, six, including himself, rode with one leg. The others wore a prosthetic leg and the racer from Spain was a double below-the-knee amputee who also wore prosthetics.

The forty-five-mile race consisted of four laps around a loop of just over ten-miles, and it was by far the most complicated track Rex had ridden. As the grueling course of inclines and S-turns wove through the cobblestoned streets of the Jewish Quarter above Barcelona, Rex moved between the third and fifth positions. The homes and shops painted in muted tones of green, blue, and orange blended together like melted crayons, making the individual structures look like one long unit flanking each side of the Onyar River. A light sulfur smell invaded the autumn air. Not losing focus, he kept close to his teammate, Pier, and the fair-skinned, blonde, Austrian racer, leading the pack.

Rex pumped hard and inhaled deeply using his strength to gain standing on the hills, going into the green rolling knolls of Catalonia. Resolute on winning, he set his mind to disregard pain, no matter how intense the burning in his thigh or the spasm in his back. His biceps and triceps bulged as blood surged through his muscles.

He was encouraged by the spectators, wearing hats and sunglasses, and waving small flags on the sidewalks and along the barricades. They cheered as the racers followed arrows pointing the way through the labyrinthine of downtown, Barcelona streets. He pedaled hard in the S-turns, which shifted him from the outside of the pack to the inside within seconds, forcing him to be alert for opportunities to break away and advance his position.

By the middle of the third lap, Rex was fatiguing. He neglected to rest. He never rested enough. He knew his compulsion to overcompensate for his disability and prove

217

himself to be a worthy athlete, caused him to train too much and not give his muscles adequate time to rest and repair. Overtraining quickened his growth as a competitor, but at times lack of adequate rest would also prove to be a detriment. This was one of those scenarios. Holding strong in the third spot, for most of the race, he now felt it slipping away. It was time to make a decision: continue at his current pace or hold back to keep a reserve for the end sprint.

Ten-minutes later, the pack approached the short, steep, grade near the end of the lap, Rex decided to go for it. Knowing he was strong on the hills and that this incline was short, he gritted his teeth, stayed in the same gear and strained to pedal faster, crimson veins pulsating from his neck and forehead.

Picking up his pace gave him crucial momentum going into the climb. *I didn't come here to lose,* he began an internal pep talk, *God give me strength.* At that moment Rex reached the top and the grandeur of Montjuic Castle came into full view. Rex drew puissance from the valor of the sixteen-hundreds defense hub, and passed over the top of the hill poised, again, in the third position and descended at breakneck speed around the left bank, and into the straightaway toward the finish line gaining on the leader.

When the banner strung across the road with "Sortida" written across it in large blue letters came into sight, there was just one lap to go. Rex knew the course now: where to attack, take a drink of water, conserve energy. In spite of being tired, he began the final lap with confidence, never forgetting his competitors wanted to win as badly as he did. Like him, every one of them would lay everything on the line to claim their spot on the podium with a medal hanging over their chest.

While making another left bank through downtown, on this final lap, Rex lifted his eyes, just as he was passing a two-toned brown building, perhaps an apartment complex with commerce at street level. At the point, it formed a triangle on the corner where two streets intersected, was a glass door, directly above the door hung a sign that simply read, "Bar."

The juxtaposition of sitting on a barstool and sitting on his bike seat jolted his psyche. The divine reminder of how far he had come, told him to never forget where he had been, and that temptation lurked on every corner calling out to him like a seductress in the window. The celestial moment, like a flash, brought to mind the day he first rode a bicycle at Skeeter's house, two years ago, and sensed something big was going happening. In that split second, while racing in the 1992 Paralympics, he gained clarity of that preceding intuition.

219

Cycling was going to give him a platform on which his prayer of service would be built. He was to use it to tell his story of redemption to as many people as he could. All he needed to do was win and the doors would magically open. A new energy swelled inside of him and his leg seemed to move on its own.

For nine miles of the last lap, he hovered between third and fourth, still near Pier. The Spaniard was in the top five now, too. The pack approached, for the last time, the steep elevation just before the finish line and all the racers sped up. This was it, the final showdown to the end. The inner odyssey long subsided, his leg now heavy, like a lead balloon. He pulled up and pushed down as fast as he could, and still, it seemed like he was moving in slow motion. Grunting, he denied the excruciating pangs in his thigh and paid no mind to the fact that his arms were about to collapse.

He saw the Austrian break away and Pier followed in second place. Rex and the Spaniard, who was able to stand up and pedal with two husky thigh muscles, tussled for third. Wheezing, from his lingering cold, and consumed, Rex could not keep up and crossed the finish line in fourth place. The bronze medal eluded him by mere seconds.

Spent and diminished, he sat speechless on the ground at the staging area where he covered his face in his hands to hide the tears welling up in his eyes. The catastrophic failure ruptured the dam of his ego and humiliation flooded his body.

After twenty minutes of deep breathing, to calm his stinging nerve endings, he pulled himself together enough to gather his gear and return to the shuttle, where he sat in the back in silence, afraid if he spoke his emotional dam would burst as well. He did not want that to ensue in front of all the other athletes, now making their way on to the bus, some celebrating their victories with high-fives and showing off their prizes. Jose entered last and sat on the bench across from Rex.

"It's tough, man, I know," consoled Jose, to Rex, who was staring out the window. "I'm not going to go into a bunch of shit about snapping out of it, I just want to say this; there will come a time when you grasp just how good you did."

At the hotel, Rex went straight to his room, shut the door and sunk into depression's darkness, while what felt like a spiritual battle for his sanity and faith sieged him.

For the next two days, in the apartment or around the village, he smiled and faked it as best he could to his teammates, while the voices in his head warred against each other.

God, what about when I passed by the bar?

Who are you to tell your story, you're nobody.

How am I going to help people now?

221

You're not! Just accept that you will always be a loser.

When the torment began to lift, he called his mentor back in Colorado.

Rex told Andy that he finished fourth, that he wasn't bringing home a medal. "I let everybody down."

"Who did you let down? You didn't let anybody down. In Korea, I came in sixth and after that, I was the world champion. Rex, this was one race, one day, it doesn't measure your skills."

"It feels like it does."

"Why don't you tell me what happened?"

Rex let Andy know that when he would break away, the other riders attacked and chased after him, but when someone else broke away, the strong guys would just sit and not advance after them.

"It sounds like you were marked, Rex. Word must have gotten around about your ability," expressed Andy, capitalizing on this teaching moment. "It sounds like they wanted to wear you out and their strategy succeeded. Learn from this, you don't have to attack every time someone breaks away."

"Yeah, I learned that the hard way."

On the third day after the race and after speaking with Andy, while eating a lunch of spaghetti and breadsticks in the cafeteria, the surprising fact of how quickly and completely he could be hijacked by his mental state shocked him. As he sat alone, twirling his noodles with his fork realizing how far he still had to go in learning to control his mood swings, he shook his head disappointed that his selfishness could so easily monopolize his life. Taking a bite of his breadstick, he stared across the room at the gathering of people in wheelchairs, who burst into laughter, and silently acknowledged that it was an embarrassed ego that sent him into a tailspin over not placing in the top three.

Get over yourself, you're fourth in the world, he caught himself saying audibly and felt joy return to his soul. He flagged down a server and ordered another plate of spaghetti to carbo load for the next day's training ride. Turning his attention back to the paraplegics, he knew deep down that if he didn't find a way to bridle his emotions and stay connected to his higher power, he would use again, and that stark truth scared him.

25

MOUNTAIN BIKING

His first day back to the Community Care Center, Rex relaxed into his chair, stretched his arms over head and leaned back, reacquainting himself with the old familiar space. Gazing at the faded impressionistic garden picture, he snickered as he thought about how something so ugly could be seen as beautiful, and end up on the wall as decoration. Still elevated from the Paralympic experience, his office seemed unremarkable; but there was no other place he would rather be.

He opened the center drawer of his desk, amidst the pens, paper clips and sticky pads, set a white key tag that read "Welcome." It was one of many he acquired over the years from Narcotics Anonymous. He rubbed his thumb over the worn plastic and turned it over. On the back was a small sticky smudge, remnant of the phone number once taped there. An NA cliche' ran through his mind; "If we call the Dope Man instead of the Hope Man, we can throw this key tag in the gutter & our ass will soon follow."

"Rex, Rex is that you? Are you back?" Rex heard a slightly slurred voice coming from the hallway.

"Yeah buddy, it's me," said Rex, as Stephen, a mentally challenged patient, appeared in the doorway. "Come in, sit down."

"I saw your door open, welcome back." Stephen clumsily sat down.

That old NA saying resonated in Rex's heart, as he watched Stephen walk into his office. At that moment, he realized that he had become a Hope Man. Feeling blessed, tears welled up in his eyes.

"When did you get back from racing your bike?" Stephen leaned forward.

"I got home two days ago."

"Are you glad to be home?" asked Stephen, his eyes staring at the white plastic object twirling around Rex's finger.

"I sure am, buddy. I sure am."

"I'm glad you're home, too," said Stephen, leaving as quickly as he came in.

Rex placed the key tag back in the drawer and thought, *my office may be dull but there's nothing ordinary about this job.*

***

Taking a break from training on the road, Andy suggested mountain biking as a much-needed change. They planned a day for Andy, Marc and Brad to meet Rex at White Ranch, a popular front range mountain biking destination in the Rocky Mountains.

"This ought to fit you all right. There's no rear shock absorber, it's a hardtail. So it might hurt a little going over jumps." Andy rolled the bike to Rex, continuing to point out that being on the dirt has a lot more variables to be aware of; rocks, crevices, tree limbs, mud. "You can lose your balance real easy out here."

"Well, if I fall, it won't be the first time."

"There are water bars, said Marc, explaining that logs are laid across the trail to divert water off of the path, and they can be pretty tricky until you know the trail. "You don't know how big of a jump you'll have to make until you're already flying over it."

"OK. I'm ready!"

"Let's go! Enough of this tea party. Maverick Trail is this way." Marc waved for the group to follow.

Riding over the ruts and rocks made for a bumpy ride, jarring Rex's ribs as he ascended up the main climb with his riding buddies. Keeping his balance was nearly impossible as he bounced across the rugged path, which caused him to put his foot down every twenty feet. It was one thing to be told about it, but another to find out for yourself how much difference there is between biking on and off the road. He was immediately enthralled with this whole new arena to conquer. On the inside, underneath all of his frustration from learning a new skill, he was smiling; road cycling is next to nature, this put him right in the middle of it.

Halfway back to the bottom, riding more carefree, Rex pedaled faster and faster down the swampy Maverick Trail. Camouflaged by mud, Rex didn't see the pit that abruptly stopped his front tire at the top of a twenty-foot slope. The sudden halt sent him sailing over the handlebars and tumbling down the hill, his bike crashing end over end beside him.

"Oh shit! Rex, you OK?" yelled Marc.

Rex did a quick self-assessment. "Yeah. I think so."

"Those mud traps are a bitch. You need some help? I mean you're way down the bank."

"I got it. I'm good." Rex wiped mud from his face.

"Are you sure? That was ugly. Sorry, man, I don't mean to be laughing, but nice superman! You hit that hole with your front tire and endo'd over the handlebars. I thought for sure you broke your neck."

"You look like you just got out of a mud bath," Andy chimed in.

"Yeah, some mud bath, all right," said Rex still wiping his forehead.

"Take your time," said Andy. "We'll wait. I'm with Marc, though. I thought you were going to be an organ donor. I'm glad you're all right because that was pretty funny."

"Glad I could provide the day's humor for everyone," said Rex, as he stood his bike upright and faced his friends staring down at him.

He slogged up the mucky slope, lifting the bike, moving it forward two feet, holding on to the frame and hopping up next to it, then repeating.

"A little mud never hurt anybody, my skin is already softer. Everyone ready?" asked Rex when he reached the top.

228

"That's the attitude. This is a lot different from being on the road, isn't it? Maybe I'll try a mud facial too," said Coach Brad, flicking a clump off of Rex's shoulder. "Oh, that kind of crash, it's called a biff!"

In love with mountain biking, Rex spent just as much time on the dirt trails as he did on the paved road. His skill level rose and he quickly made a name for himself among the mountain bikers.

One day, Rex and Jeff, his amputee friend, met at the Castle Trail on Mt. Falcon, where they often rode together. Purple locoweed, copper mallow and prickly pear cactus flanked the exposed single track with pops of purple, orange and yellow. The mid-spring sun warmed the back of their necks.

"I'm not holding anything back today. No choking. I'm going to get to the top of this sucker in less than fifty minutes."

The two headed up the Castle Trail ready to conquer the 2500 vertical feet.

"Yeah? Today's the day, huh? Jeff lifted up on the handlebars and bounced his front tire a couple of times.

"Yep, if I don't die first."

"I'll be the first one to talk it up. Do it under 50 and you'll be Mt. Falcon famous," boasted Jeff.

229

"Yeah, yeah." Rex pushed in the tiny black timer knob on the side of his watch.

"I can hear it now, 'the dude with one leg made it under 50'."

The two stayed close and made good time, riding clean all the way through the first series of water bars and around the first switchback. The incline turned into an eighteen percent grade that devoured the inexperienced and made even the best riders switch to an easier gear. Rex's chest burned with each breath of thin high altitude air, however, he wasn't ready to down-shift, determined to break the fifty-minute mark.

"Push through, man. You can do it. You just gotta push through," Rex encouraged Jeff when he saw him shift gears.

"I'm gassing, man," said Jeff, his back hunched over.

"Come on, we're almost there. Dig in!"

"Damn it, if you can do it, so can I," Jeff said, shifting up.

"You can, too," said Rex to another rider, who was holding onto a tree branch, resting.

"Thanks, man, I will," replied the out-of-breath rider, whose eyes widened as he noticed Rex only had one leg.

As much as Rex wanted Jeff to stay with him, this was no day to hang back. Rex knew the nuances of the trail and was prepared. He sat a little lighter on the seat when he came to the rock garden studded with large stones making it difficult to ride through. Thankful his new bike was equipped with double suspension, he crossed the jarring terrain with confidence.

Squeezing the handlebars a little tighter, he knew how fast to take the switchbacks. It was a delicate combination of speed and balance. Determined not to put his foot down, he placed his hand on the side of the mountain to steady himself around the particularly tight corners. Inches from the mountain wall, he could see coffee and oatmeal-colored strips of dirt filled with specs of something glittery. His hand dragged along the soil on the mountain and knocked off tiny green plant life stretching toward the sun.

Focused on his goal, doubt did not interrupt his train of thought while crossing the tight sequences of water bars and jumps almost impossible to traverse without downhill momentum, all the while dodging branches and being mindful of other riders, able-bodied, who nodded as he passed them by. The bouts of shade were welcomed, but brought little relief to his sunburned nose.

Sweat-drenched and panting, he sped up to the brick columned gazebo at the top, and stabilized himself on the picnic table in the middle. The timer on his watch read 00.48.27. Staring down at the numbers in disbelief, a drop of moisture trickled from the tip of his nose and landed on the glass, blurring the digits. He wiped it off with the bottom of his T-shirt, careful not to disturb the clock. A wave of satisfaction washed over him.

He gazed out over the canyon where the sun cast alternating hues of violet and turmeric across the rolling hills. Snow patches still clung to the north facing sides. A cool drink of water soothed his throat, dry from dust and exertion. At that moment, time stood still. He felt as if there were a singular pulse of energy, an interconnectedness that joined him to this magnificent network of beauty residing before him. No longer just a witness to the majesty, he was a part of it and he understood the enormity of God.

Jeff rode up to the gazebo, the sound of his tires rolling over twigs and leaves, disrupted Rex's spiritual encounter. Not wanting to leave this newly found space, Rex savored one more deep breath before acknowledging his friend.

"Hey, what's your time?"

"Fifty three minutes and 19 seconds." Jeff rolled up to Rex. "What's yours?"

"Forty eight, twenty seven."

"Congratulations, man. You did it!"

"Yeah, I conquered this sucker!" Rex reached into the pouch attached to his bike frame and asked Jeff if he wanted a protein bar. The two sat on the bench replenishing some calories and recharging in the shade.

"Hey, you made it," said Jeff to the rider they passed earlier

"Just barely. That climb kicked my ass," said the rider rolling up to the table.

"Rex made it under 50, this guy's incredible," raved Jeff.

"My hats off to you man. That's awesome!"

Word spread through the mountain biking community that Rex rode Mt. Falcon in under fifty minutes. Although he knew people talked about him, he shied away from the accolades in person. Like at the Community Care Center, this was another area where he could be a Hope Man. In the parking lots, at the trailheads, on the mountains, he would notice people gawking at him, whispering. He knew they were wondering if it was him, the crazy guy with one leg, agile, fearless, strong. The man who scaled the mountain, like a Billy Goat.

***

It was the spring of 1993, less than a year since Barcelona, when Rex opened his front door after work and heard the phone ringing. He debated whether to answer it or not. It had been a full day at the Center, and the first morning of the new training plan Andy and Brad structured for him. Hoping they would hang up, he decided not to answer it. After the fifth ring, it went to the answering machine. "Hey Rex, It's Jo...." Rex grabbed the receiver, "Hello."

Jose was calling to tell Rex that the Paralympic cycling coaches brainstormed a plan to pool the resources of the classifications and put amputee, blind and Cerebral Palsey riders under one umbrella. Peter sent in a proposal to the National Governing Body, the NGB, and it was accepted. The coaches were given the green light to form a team and have access to the Olympic Training Center in Colorado Springs.

Jose told Rex he was mailing him an application to fill out and send in to the NGB, and that they would be getting the training facility this summer when the Olympics weren't using it.

"Are you asking me to be on the team?"

"Yes, I'm asking. I'm the coach for amputees and I want you on my team."

Rex sat down to take in the great news. Instead of relishing in joy, he found himself confused. He picked up the nearest junk mail envelope and began to journal, a recovery tool he used often.

What is causing this? How can this mood swing happen so fast? I talked to Jose on the phone and was ecstatic about the news of being on the team and the training camp. Why do I feel like shit now? Is it because I was up so early and I'm tired? Maybe that's part of it, my defenses are down. It's more than that, for some reason I feel unworthy. What a bunch of crap. I'm so fucking tired of banging my head against this wall. Now, I'm getting pissed and that's not good either. Luckily, the meeting is tomorrow. I need a reality check. I'm just going to take a shower and go to bed. Five o'clock is going to come early again. Don't fuck this up!

The next evening Rex went to his meeting as he did every Tuesday.

"Hi, I'm Rex and I'm a drug addict."

"Hi, Rex," responded the group.

"Great news! I was invited to officially be on the Paralympic cycling team. Bad news, I'm afraid I'm going to screw it up. It's those old tapes playing in my head, you know." Rex asked the group to hold him accountable, and as usual, when he finished sharing, the power of those old demons that still come back to taunt him, was extinguished. Rex ended by telling the new people, "speaking your shit out loud works."

235

26

FIRST DAY OF TRAINING CAMP

Check-in time wasn't until 4:00 pm, so Rex worked a half day at the Center to repair leaking faucets and straighten up his office. Like a high schooler in last period, he was having a hard time concentrating, and glanced at his watch every two minutes, surprised that more time hadn't passed. Finally, he signed out, and his coworkers wished him well going to his first official training camp.

Sitting in the cab, Rex peered over his shoulder into the bed of his truck, checking one more time that his bicycle was secure. When he turned back around, he saw himself in the rear-view mirror. Having processed his initial reaction to the news of being chosen for the Paralympic cycling team, with recovery friends, he paused, stared at himself and said, "this is who I am. This is my life now. Fuck all that other shit," and started the engine. The Van Morrison cassette came on loud and he belted along with the song, "Into the Mystic"

The midday temperature climbed to ninety degrees as he drove south on 25, toward Colorado Springs. Despite the heat, he rolled the windows down and let the wind swirl about the cab during his one hour and fifteen minute drive. Motoring down the freeway at 70-miles-per-hour, the bellowing hot air felt thick as it slapped his face and swung around like an angry monkey pent up in a cage. Oddly, it invigorated him. Something was fascinating and mysterious about the rushing wind.

Rex turned right off of Boulder St., into the main entrance of the training center, at about 3:30. Once in, he turned onto N. Meade Ave., and drove around the sculpture garden and down to where he saw a sign reading Paralympic Cycling. He parked and walked across a generous lawn fragrant of being recently mowed

Pier, the other above-the-knee amputee and Barcelona teammate stood waiting for Rex, along with Jose Alcala, Paralympic cycling coach. Also with them was Bob Whitford, whose right arm had been amputated . "Hey guys, the meeting is this way," said Jose.

Rex walked with Pier and Bob passed the dorms to the adjacent building, where the team gathered in the Gold Meeting Room.

"Hi everyone, welcome to the Olympic Training Center. I'm Jackson, your tour guide. I'm going to take you on a condensed tour of the complex. There looks to be about forty of us, I've arranged for a few golf carts for those that require a ride and the rest of us will walk. Any questions before we head out?"

"Can we leave our things, or should we take them with us?" asked Peter Paulding, the head coach.

"If you have belongings, you can leave them here. We'll be back in about thirty minutes."

Rex didn't need to leave anything. His pouch was attached to the rung on his crutch and he left his suitcase in his truck. He lined up with the others and followed the guide out the door, going back the way he came in.

As he strolled along with his team, it donned on him this was only the second time he was with a group of this many disabled people. The first was the games in Barcelona. There were a lot of the same athletes, he recognized some of the blind riders and stood in awe at how fluidly they moved about, scanning their white canes back and forth.

He was the only one using crutches.

"This is the Carol Grotnes Belk Sculpture Garden. As you can see it is visible from the street and one of the first things you notice when you come onto the grounds. The large bronze globe symbolizes world unity. It is being held up by four ethnically diverse, brawny men, depicting strength of the athlete. These are the life-size runners and there is a dancer...."

Rex made mental notes of the information. He wanted to be prepared in case there was a pop quiz he would have to pass to move on to the next level of being on the team, kind of like being punched for a Final Club at a prestigious college. He didn't want to be the one humiliated, although he knew it was all a silly notion.

"OK, let's move along. Follow me and we'll head down to the Olympic Pathway and Sports Center II, where you will have access to one of the weight rooms."

Rex waited for the crowd to move before joining in at the back as they walked to their next stop.

"Everything in here is brand new," explained Jackson.

There were rows and rows of different kinds of weight machines, long lines of cardio equipment and a copious free weight section with plenty of vinyl-covered benches, all facing a large mirrored wall. Rex surveyed the shiny chrome stretched across the room, and saw a stark difference from those days in the tiny hospital gym. He felt a sense of achievement.

"OK, let's head back to the Gold Meeting Room. This concludes our tour."

Peter let the crowd get settled in the meeting room before he spoke.

"So what do you think?" Peter's arms spread out wide. "Not bad, huh."

"This place is awesome!" A voice rose above the cheering team.

"This has been a long time coming, and it's because of you that we're here. Some of you I've known for a while and just met others in Barcelona, but I want you to know that it was you, your hard work and skill level, that inspired us to pursue the NGB and get the Paralympics to where it should be. You deserve it."

Applauding with the crowd as they listened to Coach Paulding make his welcoming address, Rex felt like this could be something bigger than winning races. It could be something that transcended the sport. Sitting amongst his new teammates, his thoughts drifted and allowed his dream to expand. In his mind's eye, he watched it take new form: merging his sport and his desire to help people. Vaguely aware of the rustling around him, he drifted back to when Skeeter put him on that old Huffy and the feeling in his gut on that life-changing day. He shivered as a wave of energy surged through his body.

"You know, this is the first time Paralympic cycling has been granted permission to use this facility." Peter addressed the athletes. "We are making history and through hard work and dedication, we're going to get Paralympic cycling the recognition it deserves. It won't be easy. Are you up for it?"

"Yeah" the team cheered, pumping their fists in the air.

Fully aware of his surroundings now, Rex wanted to be attached to a movement that shattered the stigma society placed on him because he only has one leg. To destroy the myth that disabilities are liabilities.

"Good, Peter continued. Because now for a little not so great news."

During the games in Barcelona, the coaches observed that, compared to the rest of the world, USA cycling was mid-range in skill set and the coaches wanted to change that. So, the first thing they needed to do is was find out the precise skill level of each team member. "You're going to be pushed until you fail, said Peter. "I believe, sadly, disabled folks get too many limitations placed on them: that isn't going to go on here. We're not concerned with what you can't do, we want to see what you can do."

As Rex listened to the pep talk, he looked around the room at everybody on the team – his team. He noticed that in the room full of physically disabled people, sitting down he appeared normal. This notion wasn't new to him. He contrived tricks to hide his missing leg. Now he almost laughed out loud: *the one place it didn't matter, and you couldn't tell.*

He appreciated Peter's words and what the coaches were doing on behalf of the cyclists, but with his new dream of serving through his sport intact and bored with the rally cry, all he wanted to do was get off his ass and ride.

27

Paralympic Training Camp

Rex stood and donned his dark blue windbreaker. Leaving not a crumb on his plate, he placed his black, plastic breakfast tray in the allotted bin and convened with the rest of the team in the cafeteria parking lot. The early morning chill jabbed his leg as he inserted the Nike water bottle into its holder on the bike frame. They were riding the short distance south to Memorial Park. Rex dreamt about competing on the velodrome since the day Jose called and invited him to the training camp.

"So, here we are at the velodrome." Head coach, Peter, addressed his team standing before him in a colorful array of

243

bike shorts and nylon jackets. "If you're scared of heights, don't look down," he smiled.

"That's no joke," Rex, sitting on his bike, looked over the rail at the steep embankment.

"Yeah, I hope it's easier than it seems," said Bob.

"Track racing is popular in Europe, as I'm sure you know. We want to incorporate it into our arsenal, as well," continued Peter. "So, this curly-headed guy, wiping his hands with a towel, is Thompson, he competes on the velodrome and works here. He'll give us an overview of what it's all about."

Rex stared at the huge oval-shaped track. The concrete appeared warped, yet smooth, glass-like. It dipped and raised, and banked. Bright red USA and the Olympic logo of blue, gold, black, green and red interlocked rings were stenciled onto the turn at the South end of the track, and solidified to Rex that this was *no joke;* this was the Olympics! The breeze nipped his cheeks as the morning sun illuminated Cheyenne Mountain. *This is the mountain top.*

"The track here at Memorial Park is 333 meters long and has a 35-degree maximum bank going around the turns. That's a little more than the steepness of a staircase." Rex listened as Thompson began to educate the team. "You'll notice, different colored lines going around the track; the wide blue band is the area between the infield and the track." Rex remembered from races he watched, that the wide blue band is not part of the track. It is only crossed to enter and exit the racing lanes.

"Just above that is the black line, or pole line," Thompson dried his hands and flung the towel over his shoulder. "It marks the beginning of the meter-wide pole lane where most of the racing is done. Above that, the red line is the outer edge of the pole lane."

"That's about as wide as a sidewalk," Rex turned to Bob.

"Yeah, not very wide," Bob answered, still leaning against the railing.

"Halfway up the track you see another blue line," Thompson continued. "That's the stayer's line. It marks a separation. So, for instance, a rider below the blue line cannot be taken on the inside, you have to go above that line to make your move. It gets pretty steep that high up on the track."

"You fall up there, your ass is going to roll for a while," said Bob.

"You got that right." Rex raised his arm in a slant to replicate the angle. "That would be a hell of a crash. I'm ready!"

"OK, that's a very basic overview. Let's go down to the infield. Follow me," directed Thompson.

"Go ahead," said Rex to Scott, another team member, who shuffled by, dragging his feet. Rex was amazed at how good the cerebral palsy team members could ride after seeing their unsteady body mechanics. He watched Scott walk to his bike, slightly bent at the waist, like he might fall forward with each step, stiff legged and barely bending his knees. Yet, when he rode he used full range of motion. There was Rex's proof; disabilities are not liabilities.

"Gather around everyone," instructed Thompson. "I'm going to go over the type of bike used on the track, it's different from road bikes."

Eager to hear what Thompson was saying, Rex made his way up to the front, using his bike as a crutch. He had been hankering for this new challenge since going over the schedule the first night at camp.

Weeks before coming, to give himself an edge, Rex began to visualize himself racing on the velodrome, and winning. He learned about the different types of races; 40k time trial, flying 1k with a rolling start, 500m sprint.

Sprinting appealed to him far more than the 120 laps of a 40k. The results of his power output test showed he was more suited for sprints. His one leg produced as much or more force

246

than both legs of an able-bodied person. So, the short sprints were where he wanted to focus, where he would excel.

He steadied himself at the front outside edge of the group, excited to be one step closer to riding on the track and adding this specialty to his repertoire. He already made up his mind that he would be a contender and do what was necessary to rank that high. He didn't say yes to the Paralympic team just to show up and lose.

"Track bikes are a lot lighter than road bikes and you can see, the sprocket is bolted to the hub of the back wheel." Rex paid attention as Thompson covered specifics. "So, there is only one fixed gear, that's why they are called fixies, and it's the equivalent of a high gear on a multi-speed bike. If the bike tire is moving - so is the pedal. Also, there are no brakes. The way you slow yourself down is to simply ride around until you come to a stop, or apply steady back pressure to the pedals, to slow the wheel, but not too much. It takes a little getting used to." Thompson stood up and pointed to a cluster of fixies. "OK, enough talking, let's get you on those bikes."

Jose held the seat stays, as Rex situated himself on the ill-fitted saddle and clicked his foot into the inch too short crank. A perfect-fitting bike was not a concern today as it was just an initial introduction to the track. He rode around the flat infield with the rest of the team, adapting to this new style of riding. Unconsciously he would relax his leg and stop pedaling. Each time, however, the pedal continued rotating and jolted him forward in his seat, prompting him to instinctively reach for the handbrake, only to be reminded that there wasn't one. *Don't get frustrated, this is brand new.* Rex crossed back and forth until he felt confident to transition onto the track.

"Jose, I'm going up now," Rex cruised by his coach.

"OK, just remember: don't stop pedaling and keep the rubber side up, I don't want any injuries today."

Rex crossed the blue band with fervor and positioned himself just above the black line inside the pole lane. He immediately noticed two things: the slant, and that it was easier than he expected. Instead of detecting a gravitational tug, he felt like his bike was sticking to the track. The faster he went the more stable the centrifugal force made him feel. Gaining confidence, he accelerated on the straight-away and cut through the warming mid-morning air that howled as it rushed past his ears.

Just as he was making his turn onto the bank, he saw Jose out of the corner of his eye waving him down to join the team exercise, and instinctively stopped pedaling. The velocity of the pedal speed barreled up through his leg and bucked him forward lifting him from the saddle. The bike sheared off the track speeding toward the infield wall.

With wide eyes, he quickly continued pedaling to regain control, similar to pressing on the gas of a skidding car. Just in time, he swerved away from the wall. The oxygen caught in his lungs escaped, deflating his chest. He slowed himself down by applying little bits of back-pressure to the pedal and slowly rolled up to the wall, stopping next to Jose.

"Always the thrill seeker," said Jose.

"I like to scare myself, life's more fun that way."

"Hang tight for a minute, we're going to form a paceline and start some drills," Jose patted Rex on the shoulder.

Rex volunteered to take the first pull, to be the front rider, while everyone else formed a line behind him. This time he kept his speed at a comfortable pace while the team got used to the new setting. He led for two laps then peeled off up the track until all his teammates had passed, then fell back in at the end of the line, ready to take his turn drafting.

At day's end, flush-faced Rex slowly made his way to where the team was gathering, just outside the arena, his chest slightly rising with each controlled breath. Excessive heat crawled up the back of his neck, clamping down on the muscles, his stomach wanting to rid itself of any contents. The seven-block ride back to the training center seemed impossible as every muscle in his body felt like lead. He sat, covered his mouth, breathed slowly through his nose and reveled in the mixture of nausea, pain and the birth of this new love-hate relationship with the track.

"What a day," exclaimed Peter. "Some of you shined out there today. I'm excited about the velodrome and the Paralympics' future with it. I know you're all exhausted, but just one fun fact before we head back." Peter informed the group that the original Madison Square Garden built in the late 1800s, was a velodrome with ten thousand seats. At the turn of the century, bike racers were the sporting stars of the time and the best racers could earn up to $150,000.00 a year, today's equivalent to about $2,000,000.00. "OK, let's go eat."

On the final day of training camp, Rex woke to a busy mind. Pulling the cotton blanket to where the soft fabric nestled against his chin, he pondered a minute to identify who these emotional passengers were and greeted them as if they were tangible friends. The interlude reminded him of the final day of his rehab season, sitting in the lobby waiting to catch the bus. Staring at his black and green bike shorts hanging on the back of the wooden chair across the room, he realized four years had come and gone. Accustomed to contradicting emotions wrestling for space in his consciousness, this time he wasn't afraid of failure.

As he dressed for the day, he paid no attention to gloom and excitement taking their turns with the upper hand. He adjusted the seams on his bright yellow jersey that were twisted around his ripped shoulders and half-tanned, thick biceps. His perfectly formed tricep protruded as he tugged on the bottom of the short sleeve. The form-fitting lycra hugged tight to his pecs, that he flexed two times each for fun. Ready for the day, he headed to the cafeteria.

While he ate his butter-drenched stack of whole-wheat pancakes, gloom pressed down on his spirit, he stayed calm, knowing that the preferred excitement would return to its place of favor. Still not buying into the interior struggle, he finished his breakfast and gathered with his team in the parking lot one last time.

"We'll ride southwest out of the city and take Cheyenne Road up the mountain," directed Peter, "It's not a long way up the mountain, but it's steep. We'll descend back down Cheyenne Road then travel north to the Garden of the Gods. It's going to be a great ride," Peter cheered on his team. "Let's go!"

Rex removed his balancing hand from Bob's shoulder and began to ratchet his pedal up and down. All that mattered was the day's ride.

251

He found an open spot behind one of the tandem bikes and, like the cerebral palsy riders, admired the courage and fortitude of the blind man sitting on the back seat, working hard, completely dependent on his sighted partner. The word *trust* burst through the dueling emotions of gloom and excitement, disintegrating them into micro particles that left his being with each exhale.

Absorbed in the trust illustration in front of him, Rex rode with his team on the surface streets, crowding the intersections with the other hopeful Paralympians on their way to Cheyenne Mountain. "Ride hard," yelled a lady, from her aqua green Ford Explorer, as she waited for the colorful parade of cyclists to pass. "Wish I was riding with you. It's a beautiful day."

The coaches plotted a route to take in the van and the team followed closely while making their way through the city streets. The smell of car exhaust permeated the air as did the sound of the morning news coming from the vehicles of people on their way to work.

Once away from the morning commuters and into a less populated area, the riders spread out single file to form a paceline and begin their routine. Rex made eye contact with Pier and gave a quick nod that he was going to fall in behind him; Pier tilted his head in return. Rex grew comfortable riding with Pier as they were in the same classification. Rex positioned his front wheel inches from Pier's back wheel. He wanted all of the practice he could get riding close and was conserving energy for the upcoming climb.

The ominous mountain loomed in front of Rex and his team, but for now, the road was flat and seemed as though the lonely stretch of narrow gray asphalt would never ascend. Rex glided along behind Pier, watching the front riders peel off one by one until it was his turn at the helm. It wasn't long after that the road began its incline. Rex knew they were being evaluated by the coaches all along the way and wanted this to be his chance to impress them: climbing was his strength. He downshifted and pedaled harder.

It's four miles. Peter said it was four miles to the top. He began his internal monologue. Don't give up, ever.

The team broke out of the paceline and into "every person for themselves" riding up the 15-percent grade. Rex's ferocious competitiveness ignited as the two-legged teammates passed him. "Come on," he silently yelled, pushing and pulling even harder, sweat saturating the back of his jersey. He didn't care about the disparity between him and some of his teammates. He wanted to be first to the top and, more so, did not want his coaches to think he was incapable. His "only four miles," chant turned into "where the fuck is the end?"

He could hear his breathing, like having his ear to a seashell listening to the sound of the ocean. It was loud and rhythmic. His lungs expanded with each inhale, causing his form-fitting jersey to stretch even tighter across his broadened chest. The muscles in his quadriceps protruded in full view as he attacked his pedal strokes. Just when he thought he could not make one more rotation, he looked up and there was half his team, waiting at the top. The finish line was in sight, it was time to pedal even harder and end strong. When he reached the top, he could rest, not now.

"That just about kicked my ass," panted Rex, when he joined his team at the top. He turned himself around and stared in amazement at the grade he just climbed, the white center-divider-stripes stretched to the horizon.

Descending was as strenuous as going uphill, in a completely different way. Ascending pushed Rex to his physical limit and required a never-give-up resolve, but not much focus on the road. Going down, Rex fixated on the centerline, the 15% decline required his full attention. Rex stayed close to the mountainside, which changed colors as he rode in and out of the shade around the tight switchbacks. Too much speed would send him sailing over the edge, however riding the brake could cause them to overheat and become inoperable. The precipitous descension demanded acute mental focus; going downhill at speeds of 20 to 30 miles-per-hour on hairpin turns was exhilarating and dangerous – and only for the fearless. The wind burned his cheeks as he pushed his previous limitations.

From the bottom of Cheyenne Mountain, the group rode north to N. 30th Street and into the magical sandstone that makes up Garden of the Gods. Rex's eye would never tire of seeing the gravity-defying Balancing Rock on one side and Steamboat on the other side of the entrance to the park. The rock formations posed proudly against the palette of sage green mountain brush and a now cloudless blue sky.

Rex's soul was immediately filled by the creation he was now amongst. At this destination, the coaches allowed the team to leisurely ride around and enjoy the environment. Rex stopped momentarily to apply another layer of sunscreen and take in the view. He sensed a palpable electric charge in the air as he mused the proud custodians of the Garden, the Kissing Camels, being magnificently dwarfed by snow-topped Pikes Peak. As if purposely carved out of the top of a large creviced sandstone, the round humps of the face to face camels jetted into the sky as they kneeled before each other, their thick lips touching. God could be the only explanation for something as beautiful and alive and peaceful as Garden of the Gods. The presence of the All Mighty was here. Rex could sense it. In that place, another contradiction surfaced: he felt small and significant simultaneously

28

LOVE

Rex walked into his office at the Community Care Center after the seven-day training camp and everything was as he left it: the striped maroon fabric chair facing the desk, angled out, his oversized, coffee-stained, ceramic mug stood proudly on the top of his desk, aroma from the vanilla candle filled the air: and yet everything seemed different. Brighter. He reached out his hand, fingers tanned from the middle knuckle to the tip, the part not covered by his cycling glove, and flipped his calendar to Monday. There were no appointments for the day, just the yellow sticky note he left for himself with a list of repairs that needed to be made. He put his keys in the center desk drawer and went out to say hello to his co-workers.

Feeling weightless and full of electricity, Rex was experiencing a whole new kind of floating as he walked down the hall. Abstract paintings that displayed shades of brown, red, green and orange all dissolving together into undefined squares, lined the hallway. The muted earth-tones were soothing against the cream- colored walls. He hadn't taken notice of the pictures before, now it seemed as though they were pulsating with his heartbeat, and the false depression he usually experienced after coming home from an exciting event was absent, as he made his way to the front.

Amelia, the petite, blonde, front desk assistant wearing bright red lipstick, greeted Rex, as he turned the corner. "Hey, Rex is back. How was the camp?"

Rex reactively raised his hand to block his eyes from the harsh fluorescent lighting of the reception area. "It was great. A lot harder than I expected. I learned a lot."

"Cool. Great to see you."

Now, on the opposite side of the building from his office, Rex continued in his float around the Center. The abstract art on these walls contained shades of purple and the lighting softer than that of the reception area. Rex was hoping the second door after the break room would be open, as he made his way around the building to let his workmates know he was back. The door was open.

"You're here and not in a session," Rex said to Anita one of the licensed clinical social workers. "How ya doing?"

"Hey, Rex is back." Anita hugged Rex. "Sara, this is who I was telling you about," Anita introduced the new intern to Rex. "You better be nice to her," jabbed Anita.

"Me, not nice? Now, why would you say a thing like that." Rex, unable to take his eyes off of Sara, stretched his hand out.

"Nice to meet you." Sara's thick raven hair framed in her rosy cheeks and brown eyes. "So you compete in the Paralympics?" Her smile, as bright as the lights in the reception area, lit up her cherubic face.

"Yeah, we first just had…we just had our first training camp. Wow, that was smooth." Rex and the two ladies laughed.

"Well, thanks for saying hi. We've got a patient coming in. I'll let you know if we need anything," said Anita.

"OK, see you girls around," Rex turned to leave and smiled at Sara one more time. "If you need anything just let me know. Yep… you… just said that."

It was clear now, the reason for his buoyancy, as if his spirit knew before he did that a whole new emotion was going to manifest; love at first sight. *Who was that?*

After the third time he dropped his screwdriver while repairing the up and down lever on a broken office chair, Rex pounded his fist on the floor. Befuddled, he decided to get something to drink. While walking the normal way he would go to the break room, he felt a pang in his gut. It grew stronger, as he moved closer to the office where Sara was. He stopped for a moment, breathless and still. *Wow!* He looked around to see if he'd been caught, in what, he wasn't sure, aside from the fact that he was just standing in the hall by himself for no reason. His lungs released making a loud *chu* sound. *Shit! I hope nobody heard that. What the fuck is going on?* He stood frozen again, not making a sound and after a few seconds turned and went the long way around to the break room, where Sara was pouring herself a cup of coffee.

OK, just be cool. Rex couldn't take his eye off of Sara's ass. "That sure smells good."

"Hey, it's our resident Paralympian." Sara held up her cup of coffee. "Hazelnut."

"Hazel what?"

"Nut, Hazelnut."

"You're a nut?"

"And he's funny. Gotta get back to work." Sara accidentally bumped into Rex as she went out the door.

Rex stood in the doorway and watched Sara's hips sway back and forth in a smooth, rhythmic fashion, as she walked down the hall. She turned and smiled just before rounding the corner. Sighing, Rex sat down at the table and rested his chin in his hands, forgetting he was there for coffee. Attempting more repairs, but not completing one, Rex called it a day a half-hour early.

The summer sun was still high as Rex drove home. Upon pulling into his driveway, he sat and listened to the end of the song "Living on the Edge," bobbing his head to the beat before turning off the engine. He was hoping the music would help separate his day at work from his bike ride, but when the song ended, he was still thinking about Sara.

The long day allowed him to ride well into the evening. During the ride, he thought about meeting Sara, the electricity he felt in his body, and his inability to concentrate. He turned down roads he didn't normally take, trying to make sense of how quickly his life seemed to be changing, again. *Wait, nothing has changed.* His thoughts negotiated, one fighting for familiarity, the other demanding evolution. This battle always preceded a leap into the unknown. Life was the same for now, although he knew meeting Sara was going to change his life, he just didn't know when or how.

His mind was swirling thinking about the times in the past when he thought he was in love. Those times were merely lust disguised as love, blurry in the haze of addiction. This was different. He was different: sober, in recovery, a professional cyclist, a counselor. More mature and more humble, Rex wanted to know her and not just have sex with her.

He continued to ride as the sun was setting over the Rockies, the bright orange sky graduated to a light coral with punches of intense yellow shining through the thin clouds. He liked the warm sensation in his heart and noticed that there was a heaviness, too. "I'm not sad. Not depressed. Not lonely," Rex checked off feelings, inventorying himself as he headed home. With his back now to the sunset, the sky was dimmer, and he could see the stars faintly peaking out from the heavens.

The words "heaviness" and "heavens" rolled in front of his eyes like on a teleprompter. The letters were similar, he couldn't help thinking they were connected, even though, to him, their meanings seemed opposite.

The ride didn't clear his mind; it was still whirling, trying to figure the meaning out. He turned down his block just as the sun dropped below the mountains. The sky was darkening, and the faint voice from deep in his interior whispered. "It's not heaviness. It's longing. Your heart is longing for authentic love."

He slept deeply that night, cradled in the warmth of this new emotion, this ally, that unexpectedly felt more like an old friend than a new companion.

The next morning, Rex hurried straight to his office to prepare for his first mentor session. Three patients were scheduled. Thinking about his break after the second meeting made his stomach flutter. Finally, the two hours passed and Rex could leave his office. He went straight to Anita's room.

"Hey ladies, I just came by to say hi and I wanted to tell Sara; try not to bump into me today, while you're out walking the halls."

"Wait a minute, you bumped into me."

"No, after I thought about it for a while, it was definitely you who ran into me. So, I'm letting you know, I am on my way to the break room, so, do me a favor and watch where you're going."

"Ah, some more of funny Rex," smirked Sara.

The heightened sense of energy running through his body caught Rex off guard again as he made his way down the hall, passing by the now very familiar abstract artwork. He searched desperately for the proper mental compartment to store this pleasure, but it couldn't... wouldn't be harnessed. It was wild, free, uncontrollable, it made him giddy. He wanted more of it, even though the idea of exploring it scared him. He asked his sponsor to meet with him before the night's fellowship.

Rex pulled into the parking lot at 6:00 to meet with Stan, his sponsor, before the evening NA meeting started. Knowing there would be somebody setting up, he went inside and poured himself a cup of coffee. He held the white styrofoam cup to his mouth and with pursed lips blew on it before taking a drink. When he saw Stan walk in, the butterflies began to tickle inside his belly. Just the thought of telling someone about Sara made him blush.

"Sorry, I'm a little late. You have me intrigued. Your voice is different," Stan bent down the small silver handle on the coffee pot and filled his cup.

"Yeah, it's big all right and it's scaring the shit out of me. I met a girl." The men moved to a corner of the room and Stan listened as Rex shared, that upon meeting Sara, he detected a feeling or physical sensation he could only describe as a vortex of tingling energy in his body. It invaded him and he wasn't sure what it was, because how could he be in love with someone he just met.

"Sounds like you're infatuated, brother."

"It's all new to me, man. I've never been in a relationship without drugs."

"Proceed slowly my friend and be smart. If this goes anywhere, you're about to find out that nature's love is better than any drug-induced high out there." Stan nodded toward the crowding room. "Let's join the group."

Rex heard the people talking during the meeting, but when it was over, he had no idea what they were saying. His head was full of thoughts gyrating like the shiny chrome spokes on his bike wheel. *How do I handle this? I don't want to blow it? What if she isn't interested? Can I handle the rejection? Where will I take her on our first date? Will she judge my past? Am I good enough? Will she be OK with my body?*

The words spun around in his mind, too fast to catch. He drove home after the meeting with the radio off, letting his thoughts have their way.

Upon coming into the house, Rex threw his keys on the kitchen counter and went to his room. The springs in his bed creaked as he sat on the bottom edge and pulled off his worn down sandal. He lay back and stared at the ceiling, trying to remember the meeting; it was a blur. He shrugged it off, and began to write in the spiral-bound notebook he called his journal.

This is fucking crazy, I'm thrown for a loop. I gotta sort this out. What is this love shit anyway? I gave up on it, believing I'm not capable of healthy love. Now what? Maybe I am. I don't even know how to describe what's going on. What Stan said was cool, "that love when right sloughs off things that are unnecessary and enhances what is already good." Well, that sounds well enough, but what the fuck does it mean? Like how does that work in real life? I have more questions than answers. It's just that now all of a sudden, there is a new thing that's important to me. Well, I have to see where it takes me. Real love, who would've thought. Oh, guess I should put the date, August 1993.

29

SPONSORED

Rex propped up the pillows on his bed and lay back on the dark brown blanket. He held his new Cannondale jersey to his face, overwhelmed at what having a sponsorship represented; success, financial support, credibility, respect. The fresh-smelling polyester felt soft against his cheek as he inhaled slowly, savoring the moment.

"Rex, they'll want to sponsor you," answered Andy, when Rex argued they wouldn't want to sponsor a guy with one leg. "That is precisely why they will." Andy's words echoed as Rex zipped up the jersey and tugged on the stretchy band around the bottom of the garment. "The level you compete at, Rex, with such an obvious disability will make it easy for them. How many medals have you won in the year since the Paralympic training camp? Just call them."

Thankful he had listened to Andy, Rex studied the way the long horizontal pocket across the lower backside was sewn. Two vertical seams were attached, spaced evenly across the pouch turning one long pocket into three smaller compartments, where he would store his protein bars and car keys on training rides. He clasped the top edge of each pocket between his forefinger and thumb and pulled outward causing the elastic to snap when he quickly released his fingers.

Four years after meeting Andy at the children's hospital fundraiser ride, Rex felt indebted to his mentor. Now, because of Andy, Cannondale was Rex's first cycling sponsor. He decided the best way to repay Andy was to keep winning. Rex called Sara to tell her the good news.

"Hey, baby, my bike came!" Eight months had passed since Rex first met Sara. During that time he discovered his biggest stumbling block regarding Sara was him being rough around the edges and coming from humble beginnings.

"Your bike's here already?" Sara was more refined and came from a well-to-do family. Once Rex gained that clarity, he was able to push the limiting belief aside, and ask Sara out.

"Yeah, it came early. It's black, and the jersey is blue and white. It's beautiful."

"I'm so proud of you. I can't wait to see it. Not to change the subject, but don't forget lunch with my parents tomorrow."

"I'll be over after I take her for a spin." Now the opposites were in a romantic relationship supporting each others' aspirations. Rex felt a true sense of belonging as he shared with the love of his life.

Rex hung up the phone and went out to the living room where his new bike stood as the main attraction in the space. Pulling the ottoman over, Rex sat down and stared at the large white block letters of the Cannondale emblem stamped up the center of the aluminum frame.

The overhead light caused the polished, black metallic paint to dazzle and make starburst patterns that jumped off of the bike into the air. The metal was cold on Rex's fingers as he ran his hand across the letters and up the titanium seat posts. Long gone were the days of borrowed bikes that resembled strung together beer cans, *this is a fucking rocket ship.* He chortled at the $2,525.00 price tag, *I have my very own rocket ship and it was given to me. I won't let them down.*

With a full heart, Rex inspected every inch of his new bike. Studying each component as if cramming for an important exam. He lightly tugged on the cable housing arched out from the cable adjustment box on the Shimano derailleurs, and used the bottom of his shirt to rub the smudge off of the shiny silver CODA crankset and checked again that the left one had been removed.

Bursting with excitement, he breathed slow and rhythmically to settle himself. He wanted to call Sara again and share this moment with her. Instead, he squinted his right eye and cocked his head left to eyeball the Vetta TT saddle. Even though he knew he could not see if the micro measurements of its placement were right for his body. He pushed down two quick times on the black leather covering, testing the firmness of the foam seat. *One hundred miles in and this will fit like a glove.*

When he came to the Syntace C2 carbon handlebars, he stood, paused and slowly wrapped his fingers one at a time around the black grips and squeezed. They felt strong and sturdy in the palms of his hands. He felt strong and sturdy as he inspected the discolored skin around his elbow and forearm, one of many road rash scars on his body. Seeing the blemish triggered memories of the times he pushed through when he thought he had nothing left to give, and of the lonely hours of just him, his bike and the road that seemed to never end.

Now squeezing each brake lever slightly, then harder, his mind continued in this sort of trance, recalling the victories over the ever-present mental antagonist whose seductive ways if left unchecked would destroy everything he worked so hard for. Rex's emotions surged and he sat holding his chin in the palms of his hands as hot tears cascaded down his cheeks and onto his lips. He licked his upper lip tasting the salty droplets.

He wiped his eyes on his T-Shirt sleeve and rose to go to his room. At the hallway entrance, he stopped and turned to gaze, through watery eyes, at his new bike. *I'm sponsored. I can't believe I'm sponsored.*

Just as the morning sky glowed amber, fitted in his new jersey, Rex adjusted his helmet strap underneath his chin, clicked into the pedal and pushed off from his truck ready to christen his new rocket ship with a short thirty-mile ride. Praying while he rode was so automatic now that his mouth began to move on its own as he pushed and pulled on his right pedal making his way down the block.

"God, thank you for bringing me to this place in my life. I know I have not made it easy for you."

Gratitude filled his heart as he rode past the crystalized lawns and slivers of light shining through kitchen window curtains, on a bike made just for him. His new bike was so smooth and perfect that his ride turned into fifty miles without him realizing it. He returned home just in time to take a quick shower and head over to Sara's house.

"Hey honey, it's me," yelled Rex as he walked into Sara's house. She was in the living room wrapping her father's birthday present.

"What did you get?" Sara was tying a bow on a square package.

"It's the latest Michael Crichton novel. I never know what to get my dad for his birthday. Anyway, we better be going. Tell me all about your new bike on the way," Sara kissed Rex on the lips.

"You know, one of these days you're going to marry me." Rex pulled Sara close and kissed her again.

Rex, still nervous to be around Sara's family, let her open the large wooden front door and lead the way. The high-gloss, caramel-swirled marble floor went on and on as they walked toward the kitchen, Rex careful not to put too much pressure on his crutches and leave a splotch on the luxurious tile.

"Hi you two," said Sara's mother. "Go on into the family room, dad is in there." Rex waited for Sara to go first, then followed. He glanced at himself in the hall mirror and quickly straightened his collar before entering the room. He wanted to look as proper as he could in front of Mr. Sandmin.

Sara hugged her father and placed the gift on the mantle. Rex extended his hand, "Looking good Rex," Mr. Sandmin shook Rex's hand.

Just as Rex was about to sit down, Mrs. Sandmin called out from the kitchen. "Lunch is ready."

The smell of barbecued rib eye wafted by Rex's nose and suddenly he was starving. He could hear the clinking sounds of food being placed on the dining table.

Rex sat in his chair at the end of the ornate mahogany slab. The Sandmins kindly gave him a seat where it would be easy to store his crutches against the wall. The heavy fork felt substantial in his hand, the delicate cream-colored china plates with lace patterned etching adorned the table. His setting did not include a wine glass. Mr. Sandmin sat down to the right of him.

"Mama, this spinach and strawberry salad sure looks good." Mr. Sandmin said to his wife, then leaned his large torso toward Rex and winked. "She's got us on a health kick." Rex smiled and waited to see which fork Mr. Sandmin would pick up. "Sara tells me you just got your first sponsor."

"Yes, Cannondale is sponsoring me. My bike came yesterday." Rex picked up the small fork furthest from the plate. "I took her for a spin this morning."

The butler removed the salad plates and served the main course of rib eye topped with portabella mushrooms, roasted red potatoes sprinkled with thyme and steamed asparagus.

"This is my kind of health kick." Rex cut into his still sizzling steak.

30

THE AXA CALL

Rex's cycling resume included his fourth place from Barcelona in 1992, a first place in the 1993 Disabled National Championships and second and fourth place finishes at the 1994 World Championships in Belgium. Toward the end of 1994, his notoriety gained the attention of an executive in the USA Cycling organization who was on a task force organizing a ride around the world with AXA Insurance Company.

"You want me to ride my bike around the world? Where do I sign up?" Rex blown away by being asked to join this team.

"Rex, we're thrilled to have you on our team. It's going to be an extraordinary journey," said the AXA executive, in a monotone but genial voice. "I'm glad you're as passionate as we are in wanting to show the world, through cycling, that there is a lot of *able* in disabled."

Goosebumps tingled Rex's arms as he envisioned riding his bike around the world. "We're still working out logistics. You'll be updated continually on our progress. AXA could not be more proud to be a sponsor of you and your cycling career. Welcome aboard!"

Dumbfounded by the conversation that took place, Rex sat perfectly still on the rounded arm of the dark-brown corduroy couch until he could process the information. His outstretched right leg rested on its heel and his left arm hung limply over the middle bar on his crutches where his pouch was attached. All he could think was *this is the chance of a lifetime.* The goosebumps returned and he shivered involuntarily. He slid into the corner of the couch, laid his crutches down and inspected the crease of his elbow. There were bright red indents on his skin where his arm laid heavy on the crutch bar and the straps to his pouch dug in. *They picked me because I'm good. Because I'm a winner! I have something to offer.*

"What a fucking horse-shit of a day," his roommate Skeeter barreled in the door.

"Hello to you, too," Rex shook his head, jerked from his thoughts. "What happened?"

"Ah, I don't want to talk about it right now. It's not worth the energy it would take to move my lips. What's up with you?"

"I just got invited to ride my bike around the world."

Rex told Skeeter how one of the Suits from USA Cycling, who had been tracking him, gave his name to AXA, and an organizer just called him. AXA was embarking on a big campaign to spread awareness about disability. Rex felt proud, owning his status in the disabled cycling world, and the fact that he was now a role model. "You know, it was you who put my ass on a bike in the first place."

"Buddy, you have come a long way!"

Rex furrowed his brow as he felt a twinge from the part of him deep inside that didn't want to forget where he came from. Sometimes believing in himself and acknowledging what he had accomplished, while not falling prey to pride, was a high-wire act of which he did not want to lose his balance.

A week later he received his first information packet:

...AXA World Ride is a 12,549-mile ride around the world to promote the ``able" in ``disabled." The 14-stage world ride will begin in Atlanta, Georgia, on March 17, 1995. We will travel across Europe, Russia, Siberia, China and back to the United States, concluding in Washington DC on November 18 at the steps of the Lincoln Memorial. The seven riders are:

When Rex saw his name on the list, his breath balked; this was real and immense. So far, though, he focused only on the excitement, not the planning or leaving. Eight months was a long time to be gone. He finished reading the correspondence, which made clear that it was the responsibility of each team member to contact their local media for promotional interviews.

Rex jutted out his chin and rubbed his thumb and index finger along his jawline. Questions paced back and forth through his mind: *Would Sara be supportive? Would the Center give me a leave of absence? How will I raise the money?* It stated in the letter that AXA paid for the trip. However, the athletes were required to maintain their home expenses while they were gone.

Overwhelmed by the daunting logistics of such a trip he prayed until a peace washed over him. His natural response of uncertainty when challenges arose was trumped when memories of past triumphs surfaced. Comforted, he knew God would help him find a way.

On his way to meet with *The Denver Post* reporter, Rex stopped to fill up his gas tank. Affixing the latch on the nozzle to keep the fuel pumping, he let go of the handle and leaned against the tailgate. The smell of gasoline permeated the air. He zipped his blue North Face jacket up to his chin and reached to the back of his neck to release the parts of his ponytail stuck inside his jacket. His breath turned to condensation and became visible as he watched the snow flurry through the air as gusts of wind whipped it in all directions. It was chaotic and serene at the same time. As fast as the flakes whirled around, there was a tranquility in the way they glided across the gas station lot. It occurred to Rex that it was a metaphor for what was transpiring in his life right now. Amid the hoopla, he was calm.

The glass wall at the entrance of *The Denver Post* reflected Rex's image, as he walked up to the turnstiles leading into the lobby. He stood upright and tall, conveying the confidence he now carried with him. With so many windows, Rex could see the snow splotch against the clear panes and streak down as he made his way to check-in.

The waiting room seemed bigger than it was, because of all of the windows. Even on the gray-skied day, it was light and airy and warm. Rex sat down facing the street and continued watching snowflakes mash against the window.

John Hutchinson a medium-built man with light-brown-shoulder-length hair came to greet Rex. "My office is right over here." Rex followed John to his office, ready as ever for this interview. "Have a seat, I'll be right back with some coffee."

Rex sat down and balanced his crutches on the wall behind him.

He took his coat off and hung it on the back of the chair next to him, retrieved the Chapstick from the pouch attached to his crutch and rubbed it across his cracked lips.

To pass this awkward time of being left alone in a stranger's office, Rex fidgeted with the stack of yellow sticky notes on the desk, then bent forward to read Paul's day calendar, Thursday, January 26, and there saw his name scribbled in the 3:30 slot. Rex Patrick, World Ride. He pressed against the blue tweed fabric chair back, locked his fingers behind his head and arched. He turned his chin side to side and his neck popped two times.

"Here you go," John handed Rex his coffee, steam rising from the top. "So, the World Ride. Let's talk about that," John placed a tape recorder on the desk and pushed the on button, a small red dot lit up.

"When does the ride officially start?"

280

"March 17, in Atlanta."

Rex's hands felt warm cupped around the tan cardboard cup while Paul quickly went through his first series of questions, stopping once for a drink of his coffee.

"OK, all of the formality questions are out of the way. You gotta have the facts. Now, tell me about your background? What happened with your leg?"

"Well, for most of my life I abused drugs. One day I was in no shape to drive, but my boss called me in to deliver a load of hay. The hay never made it to its destination. I fell asleep and crashed, resulting in weeks in the hospital and the amputation of my left leg."

The information flowed out of Rex like he was talking to an old friend. There was something, maybe a kindred hippieness, about John that he connected with. Whatever it was, Rex felt at ease.

"How old were you?"

"I was 17."

"That must have been a tough rehabilitation?" John sipped his coffee and leaned forward.

"Yeah, I slipped further into addiction, was homeless for a while living down at Triangle Park. I was pretty hopeless." Rex wondered again, why it was so easy to talk to this reporter. *Maybe he's in the program.*

"At some point you found recovery?"

"After a lot of tries, seven-years ago, I was finally able to stay clean and sober."

"What part did cycling play in those early years of sobriety?"

"It gave me something to focus on and get some exercise at the same time. There's nothing like fresh rocky mountain air when you need to clear your head. It's a very spiritual thing for me, as is competing."

"Now, here you are, asked to be on the team that is going to ride their bikes around the world with the mission of putting a different face on the word disability." John looked down at the press release he placed in front of him.

"Yeah, I still can't believe it sometimes. It's an honor." Rex noticed a ray of sunshine streaking through the space between the edge of the window blind and the wall. It cast a yellowish band across the L- shape part of John's desk and illuminated a photo of John holding up a large rainbow trout. *A fellow fisherman.*

"What is one personal accomplishment you want to get out of this?"

"Well, I discovered early on that if you have a physical disability people automatically think you have a mental handicap, too. Like they're the same thing. And, I think there is an automatic inclination to coddle people with disabilities. Like we can't do anything. I hate that. Those are two myths I'd like to change."

"What about financing? Do you have to pay any portion of the cost?"

"No, AXA is funding the trip expenses, we still have to maintain our lives at home. Schwinn is one of my sponsors, and they have contributed $2,000 to help me with my bills at home. I have other fundraising efforts as well. Plus, some friends from recovery are organizing a benefit barbecue."

With each new question, Rex gained clarity about the meaning of being a role model. The interview became almost dreamlike as he answered the reporter's questions. The responsibility of his cycling celebrity was sinking in more and more. People were intentionally watching him. There was an expectation for him to win. Parents were talking about him to their children. As the interview continued his right leg began bouncing up and down and he wanted to say, Y*ou know, I never thought I would even live to be 34, let alone be talking to a reporter about riding my bike around the world and representing the disabled community. Man, I am fucking up for this challenge!*

"Well, that should do it. Thanks for coming in. The article will be in Tuesday's paper," John double-checked the calendar. "Yeah, January 31. You should be hearing from the photographers tomorrow. I'll walk you out."

Stopping in front of the turnstiles, John reached out his hand. "You have an impressive story. Best of luck to you in your cycling career and in all you do, for that matter."

"Thanks, man. It's been a crazy ride," Rex squeezed John's hand with conviction

31

PREPARING FOR WORLD RIDE

The light bulb flashed and crackled when Rex flipped the switch: *Oh well*. The room was dark, which was okay, he wanted to take a power nap before going over to Sara's place. He took off his sweaty sock, and tossed it onto the tan-colored carpet. Then lay back, his right leg still over the edge of the bed.

Staring at the popcorn ceiling, his mind raced; so many details. Unable to fall asleep, he went and started the shower, then came back to his room. He turned on the light atop his bedside dresser, and picked up the piece of lined paper next to the lamp.

1. Need $5,000 for home expenses.

2. Sort through stuff. Toss or give to Goodwill.

3. Pay off truck insurance.

4. Find a place to store my truck.

5. Confirm storing stuff at Sara's.

6. Do more promotional stuff.

7. Line up people to call for accountability.

8. Get some new shoes.

9. Fill out paperwork.

10. Talk to Dr. Buno.

After reading over his list again, Rex felt relieved. The task wasn't as gigantic as he first thought. He knew exactly what he needed to do and could now make a plan. Sara was being very supportive and that alone alleviated much of his anxiety. By now, the shower was hot. He tossed the paper, it glided onto the dark brown comforter, and went to clean-up.

He sat still on the shower chair with his head down, letting the water pulsate onto the back of his neck and shoulders. Closing his eyes, he rolled his head from side to side, feeling the stretch through his neck and down across his taut traps. Noticing the water had cooled a bit he reached around and rotated the knob further into the hot zone, bent all the way forward and let the steamy stream massage his lower back.

The sweet scent of the fruity shampoo filled the air as Rex kneaded his scalp with the pads of his fingertips, pressing hard around the temples. The white lather dripped down his forehead.

Reluctantly, he finished up before he wanted to, wrapped the towel around his waist and went to get dressed. He was going to Sara's for dinner. Just as he walked in her house, Sara pulled enchiladas out of the oven.

"Oh man, that smells good. I'm starved," Rex sat down at the table and leaned his crutches against the wall behind him. A week had gone by since his last home-cooked meal.

"Careful, this is hot," Sara set the pan on to the table, then leaned over and kissed Rex. "How was your ride?"

"Long."

She set out the green salad and pitcher of tea and joined Rex at the table, where he helped himself to a heaping salad and two enchiladas.

"Here is my list," he put the paper next to Sara. "This enchilada is incredible!"

Sara thoughtfully looked it over. "Your list doesn't look bad at all. There are a couple of items we can cross off right now." Sara drew a line through number three and number five and slid the paper in front of Rex.

Stuffing another big bite of enchilada in his mouth, he looked at the paper to see what Sara crossed off. When he saw that it was 'pay off truck insurance' and 'confirm storing stuff at Sara's,' he put his cheese-filled fork down and with a mouth full of tortilla, leaned over and kissed her on the lips. "How did I get so lucky?" They finished dinner and called it an early night.

Rex lay naked on the cool cotton sheets while Sara traced her finger around his stump. He didn't usually like another person to look so closely. Over time he became more comfortable with Sara and as awkward as it was at first, he wanted her to know all of him. He closed his eyes and embraced her examination.

The sensation of Sara caressing the end of his stump went from barely detectable to ticklish, as nerve endings were stimulated. Turned on by that simple act, Rex relaxed not wanting to rush the intimate moment. Sara swirled her fingertip over the end where his skin curled under and indented from the incision. She slid her tongue across the smooth, shiny scar that ran the length of the bottom of his stump. As she moved further up his inner thigh, her gentle kisses made his body tingle and twitch, causing him to moan from the intensifying ecstasy.

Rex opened his eyes to watch her nuzzle his body, her shiny black hair lay across his plumping penis. He moaned again

288

and she looked up, their eyes meeting and becoming locked in a fuzzy gaze of euphoria. He lifted from the soft down pillow, leaned forward and pulled her to him. Their bare chests pressed together. "Baby, you are so beautiful," he whispered in her ear. With one quick move, he flipped their bodies, then ran his hand down her bare stomach and between her legs.

The heat beckoned him, luxuriating in her he made himself wait, knowing this kind of rapture is a gift of sobriety.

"Baby, why do you love me?"

"Because you're wild and crazy and strong and funny and true and stubborn and you're all mine," Sara's voice sounded celestial. The dim light cast a gentle glow across her face and hair now feathered out on the pillow.

Swallowed by this love he thought he would never find, he kissed her ruby lips long and slow. Her hips began to gyrate against his hand, he pulsed his middle finger and was pleased when she gasped. When their love making was over, they slept deeply.

The alarm rang loud at 6 a.m., startling Rex. "Sara, turn off the alarm." The buzzer kept ringing, so he reached his arm over to nudge her; she was already up.

Rex got dressed and went out to the kitchen, where the smell of freshly brewed java greeted him. He poured himself a cup and sat down at the table, the dinner plates still there from the night before.

"Good morning! said Sara, who was going to work early. "I'll see you at the office at 8. Hey, if you are going to go home first, take the rest of the enchiladas."

"Oh, man, Skeeter is going to love that."

A big grin crossed Rex's face as he watched Sara walk away. *Mmmmm,* he thought and bit his bottom lip.

The enchilada remnants hardened on the plates that were left on the table the night before. Make love or do the dishes; the choice was easy. Rex gathered the plates to the sink, rinsed them and loaded the dishwasher. *I want this life.*

The day at the Center dragged on. Not that it wasn't busy, Rex was just preoccupied with making his preparations. It was rare, but today he was glad that his last patient didn't show up. Sometimes they forget or have transportation problems. He hurried home to get a quick ride in before going to his Tuesday night meeting. His home group was well underway with planning a barbecue fundraiser for him, and he wanted to find out how it was going.

"Hey, there he is." Bobby was standing at the coffee station stirring sugar into his decaf when Rex walked in. "So,

Rex, to date we have thirty people coming to the cook-out, paying $50.00 each, and I've got fifteen more to follow up on."

"No shit! Wow. I don't even know what to say." Rex bumped his cup, the hot liquid spilling onto his finger. "Ahh," he quickly put his finger in his mouth. Calculating the math in his head, he estimated that would be more than enough to cover his bills at home.

It's going to be great! A lot of people love you, brother." Bobby squeezed Rex's shoulder.

Deeply touched by the generosity of his recovery friends, Rex teared up. Another opportunity of a lifetime and his new family wasn't going to let him miss out.

When Rex returned home from the meeting, he thumbed through the mail he tossed on the counter before leaving. Most of it was for Skeeter. Today, however, the correspondence he had been waiting for arrived; his second letter from AXA.

Rex Patrick,

We are pleased to announce our traveling schedule is in place and there are just a few more in-country logistics to be worked out. As you can imagine, the magnitude of such an endeavor takes perseverance and a great team. Due to the hometown promotion of our riders, we are gaining momentum. Many organizations for the disabled around the country have contacted us to learn more about what we are doing and how they can help. Enclosed you will find the information sheet we have put together for those companies. Also, we have included your confirmation number for your plane ticket to our kick-off dinner here in New York. The festivities will be Thursday, February 23, at the AXA offices. Attire is formal and you may bring one guest. Please confirm your reservation.

We look forward to meeting you,
The World Ride Committee.

Rex set the letter down and called Jose Alcala, his Paralympic coach, who was living in Manhattan. Rex told Jose about the AXA World Ride and asked Jose if he wanted to go to the meet and greet dinner they were hosting for all of the riders and sponsors.

"Dude, I just saw that on the news. A lot of big mucky mucks are going to be there. Yeah, man, I'll go. It'll be good to see you."

***

Rex exited his hotel into the chilly east coast evening, skyscrapers shadowing the gridlocked street, and walked the half block to 5th Avenue where he was meeting Jose at a beverage shop. Unaccustomed to wearing a suit and tie, he felt conspicuous, like he was being stared at, as he made his way down the people-filled sidewalk. He turned right onto 5th Avenue and saw Jose standing outside the neighborhood establishment. His long dark hair and thick-framed glasses were a dead give-away; otherwise, he may not have recognized Jose in his black-tie clothes.

"Hey, wow, look at you all dressed to kill," Jose's arms were spread wide.

"You're looking pretty snazzy yourself. Can you believe it?"

"Come on, let me buy you a cup of coffee and get out of the cold for a minute." Jose opened the glass door overlaid with different colored advertisement flyers.

"Thanks for coming man, I'm not used to this fancy shit."

"Yeah, me neither. I wouldn't have missed it." Jose ordered two black coffees. "This World Ride is a pretty big deal. Good for you, man."

"Yeah, I can't believe it!" Jose handed Rex his steamy drink. "This is some damn good coffee," exclaimed Rex.

"Best in the city, if you ask me. Come on, we better head over." Jose hailed a cab.

The driver dropped Rex and Jose off at the expansive and well-known Atrium at 787 7th Avenue, the entrance to the AXA building. Stepping out of the taxi, they were met by the Hare on Bell statue. A giant traditional bell made of bronze, ornamented with a tall, thin, human-like limestone rabbit suspended in the air. Long slender legs and arms extended in front and behind an equally proportioned arched torso. Its over-sized ears swept straight back as if blown by the rushing wind of mid-flight.

Once inside, the two men were saluted by another famous piece of art. The towering sixty-eight foot "Mural With Blue Brushstrokes" lavished over the minimalist and grandiose lobby.

"Wow, that's one huge painting," Rex tilted his head back to see all the way to the top of the rectangular-shaped mural. It was comprised of scenes of colorful geometric shapes and the sense of looking through a window at an oddly shaped boy holding a beach ball over his head.

Jose looked up and also considered the long vertical light blue waterfall that cascaded half the length of the mural.

The ding of one of the elevator doors opening grabbed their attention. They hurried over and stepped inside just before it closed. Rex pressed 54 and the mirrored compartment whizzed up the shaft without stopping.

Once inside the spacious, warmly-lit banquet room with panoramic views of the city, the hostess escorted them to their seats. Twenty-five round tables draped in white linen sprawled across the area, topped with blue candles flickering underneath the hurricane glasses, butter dishes and small bowls of cream and sugar.

"Mr. Patrick and Mr. Alcala." The hostess placed her hands on the Mahogany wood turn-of-the-century looking chairs and pulled them a bit from the table. "These are your seats, please help yourself to the aperitif being served across the room. Dinner will begin in about 45 minutes. Have a wonderful evening, gentlemen."

"Great, thank you. We will," said Jose.

"What did she say?" Rex asked, after she was out of earshot.

"I have know idea. Something about happy hour, maybe. Let's see what's going on over there," Jose nodded toward the gathering of people.

They walked along the west side of the hall looking out at the never-ending lights of Manhattan. They watched the activity on the Hudson River; everything seemed so small. When they got to the south end of the room, they could see the Empire State Building in the distant sky illuminated brighter than any other structure.

"Jose, let's stop here for a minute." Rex beheld the view, and stood perfectly still.

"Something isn't it, the city? The tall narrow-looking white one is Rockefeller Center," said Jose, also captivated by the view.

"Damn Jose, this is unreal. Look at me I'm standing here, looking out at the Manhattan night sky and it's pretty amazing."

"This is an incredible moment, one I'll never forget, that's for sure. Not just anybody gets to come up here."

"I'll be 35 in a couple of weeks. In my wildest dreams, I never envisioned I'd be here doing this. Things like this just don't happen to guys like me. It wasn't too long ago that I was a homeless junkie on the wrong side of Denver."

"I get what you are saying. I've gone through some shit, too. I grew up in a funky section of Detroit always having to watch my back, wondering if I'd ever get out of there."

"Yeah, now here we are dressed in suits at a party with a bunch of New York high society people." Rex steadied his crutch in his underarm and reached back to make sure the left leg of his suit pant was still securely pinned up.

"You know how I just showed you the Rockefeller Center?"

"Yeah, the white one right there." Rex pointed at the building.

"Did you see the name on the place card for the seat next to you?"

"No."

"It said, Steve Rockefeller."

"Wow." Rex hung his head and shook it back and forth. "This is all because of cycling. I'm glad you're with me, man. Come on, Jose, let's go see what kind of shit they have over there that we've never heard of."

"Sounds good. I bet Rockefeller knows what the hell aperitif means."

32

WORLD RIDE STATE SIDE

The white-noise sound of the cascading water fountain in front of The World of Coca-Cola museum, in Atlanta, Georgia, brought a balancing calm to the electricity in the air. Camera crews captured the essence in the square overrun with cyclists from every walk of life. An enormous banner hanging over the dome-shaped water feature made clear to those driving by what the hoopla was all about; it was March 17, 1995, the first day of the World Ride.

Rex clasped the straps together on his white Bell helmet as he looked around at the hundreds of cyclists who came to join in solidarity for the first seventy-four miles —from Atlanta to Athens. The fountain mist felt cold on Rex's face as he signed autographs for strangers who were taking part in this monumental occasion. Knowing they were already making an impact, satisfaction rolled through Rex's body, like a current of energy, heightening the sensation from the gust of wind that blew water from the fountain. After wiping the droplets off of his bright red windbreaker, out of habit, he reached around to the back of his head dividing his ponytail and pulling the two pieces of hair apart to tighten the band.

With his bike behind him, Rex held on to the seat with one hand and gripped the handlebar with the other hand, then leaned his butt on the crossbar. The sleeves of his light-weight jacket made a low-toned flapping sound as the breeze passed through his spread out arms. Spotting his team members, he stood and took a small jump forward with his right leg, then lifted his bike and brought it up to his butt. The crowd watched Rex repeat the quick motion, as he hopped up next to his teammates.

"Beautiful morning to ride around the world, don't you think?" Rex looked through his Scott sunglasses at Steve Ackerman, his friend and core teammate, who was paralyzed from the waist down. Steve's mirrored lenses reflected the colored jerseys of the people moving about the square.

"That it is brother, that it is." Steve looked up and smiled, his thick dark-blonde hair lying perfectly across his forehead. He reached his hand out to high-five Rex. When their palms touched Rex grasped tight, they were embarking on something very special. "Thanks again for recommending me for this ride, Rex. This means more than you know." Steve lifted his sunglasses, the genuineness shone in his steel-blue eyes.

"I know exactly what you mean. So, she's all tuned up and ready to go?" Rex shook the back left tire of Steve's three-wheeled hand cycle. It was pizza-shaped, pointy in the front and wider in the back, and low to the ground like a go-cart.

"Oh yeah." Steve pressed drown on the edges of his wide seat. "This baby might only be six-inches off the ground, but she's already taken me across mountains."

Rex hopped forward to make room for the two other core-team hand cyclists who parked on each side of Steve. Even though they seemed smaller, the hand cycles were about as long as a regular bicycle. Steve was securing his paralyzed legs stretched out on either side of the front wheel, resting on thigh, calf, and feet brackets. It looked natural for Steve to do that, Rex thought, like when he tucked his left pant leg into the waistband of his jeans. That's how life is now and would always be.

300

He watched his friend straighten his legs, then move his hands to the pedals 18-inches in front of his chest, rotating the cranks once around. Steve used his hands to pedal in the same way an able-bodied person uses their legs. *His shoulders must get tired having to hold his arms up for hours and hours;* a different perspective ran through Rex's mind. Now, double checking the chain and sprocket, Steve just leaned forward, the gears were so close to his torso. *That could be convenient.*

There was a spot behind Tour de Force champion Greg LaMonde, who joined in to ride the first leg to Athens. Rex situated himself there just as the officials stepped up and cut the ribbon at the starting line. The announcer commenced the race and wished everybody luck; the spectacle of riders flooded the busy Atlanta street.

Once the crowd of cyclists stretched out along the highway and found their rhythm of riding alongside city buses and speeding cars, Rex blended in. The gray sky made for a nice buffer against the rising sun rays, keeping them from blistering his nose and cheeks. He made small talk with different riders that ebbed and flowed beside him throughout that first day, while riding the leisure-paced seventy-four miles to their destination.

Later, the team gathered together before dinner in their hotel in Athens.

"Hey Rex, great first day, huh! Kathy, the only able-bodied person on the team slapped Rex's knee and sat down next to him. She was petite with short, dark brown hair that feathered back into a perfect wedge.

"Yep and I'm looking forward to many more ahead of us," replied Rex.

"Well, we made it through the first day! Congratulations, everyone." Paul, the ride leader and former professional bike racer, began to debrief the day. What a great turnout of support we had today, with all of the other riders."

"I felt very honored to have all of those people ride with us today," said Agnus Kirin sitting on the other side of Kathy and the only other female in the group. Her left arm was secured in two velcro cuffs, one around her forearm and the other around her wrist and attached to a thin plastic device that looked like a back brace strapped around her waist.

"I did too," said Paul, who reminded the team to always be courteous to the people who accompany them. They're going along because they care. "Each day is going to be its own thing. I will try to stay one step ahead of the challenges that will come up, but it won't always be smooth."

Rex admired Steve, who was sitting in his wheelchair across the circle, and thought about the contrast between him, the most severely disabled, paralyzed from below his chest, and able-bodied Kathy. Steve was there to show what he could do, and Kathy was there to prove that people with disabilities are worth believing in. All three of the hand cyclists impressed Rex. David wore a red helmet and carried a notebook. Another disparity thought Rex. *David has a PhD and I have a GED.* Rory McCarthy, who suffered from leg atrophy beginning in childhood, was in his wheelchair next to David. Rory had hand cycled from the state of Washington to Maine, where he worked as an electrical engineer. He always had a smile that stretched his huge mustache across his face, making it look even bigger.

"It was nice not to have any mechanical problems on our first day. Thank you, everyone, for being good to your bikes," smiled Ron, the chief mechanic, who sat next to Rex. Turning to acknowledge him, Rex noticed how easy it was to see that Ron had two missing fingers because his hand was resting on his thigh. When Ron was working on a bike it was impossible to see, as was his prosthetic left foot, because he walked so smoothly.

"Don't worry Ron, I'm sure with 8 months to go, we'll run into plenty of that," bantered Paul. "I'm sure as time goes by we will get used to the film crew, as well. We're going to have a wonderful documentary of our journey together." Paul told the group to grab some dinner and get a good night sleep, and to meet back in the same room at 7am.

As days passed, the bustle of the city gave way to the rural south. The lush greenery flanking the country roads that skirted the textile town of Spartanburg, South Carolina, was a fresh change from the tailpipes of the big city. On another day, the pink and white blossoms of the fully bloomed cherry trees in history-rich South Hill, Virginia, stood tall like onlookers at a parade. Rex and the team breathed in their fragrance as they rode through the streets of small-town America. Unlike the slow pace of riding with many guest riders, the back roads brought only a few supporters, making it possible for the team to pick up the pace. Although, still not enough for Rex. He voiced his concerns to Ride leader, Paul Curley.

"Paul, I want to ride harder. I'm going to lose fitness here and I can't afford that. I need to be ready for the Paralympics next year. At this pace, by the time we get back, I won't be able to compete."

"Rex, I understand what you're saying. I've competed myself. I'll see what I can do; I can't have you riding off and meeting us at the end of the day. Please, understand where I'm coming from." Paul's small stature disappeared behind his commanding, almost militaristic leadership style.

"When we're out there, you can't stop me from riding at my own pace." Rex's deep-rooted issues with authority were roused, and at times could still take over his personality, causing dissension between him and the team.

"That's true Rex, I can't. I'm asking you not to do that."

"I won't, I'm just blowing off steam."

"I appreciate that, Rex," said Paul, who remained calm.

By April 5, day 16, they made it to Connecticut, warm weather clothing was traded for long pants, turtle neck jerseys and heavy windbreakers. Rex shivered as he and Kathy watched the local news in the hotel lobby.

"Have you ever ridden in such cold weather?" Rex asked Kathy, the able-bodied rider.

"Windchill of minus twelve, no problem. I do it all the time!" Kathy smiled and exhaled onto the orange lenses of her sunglasses and rubbed them with the bottom of her zipped up jersey. "Clean eye protection is a must." Her eyes framed in by her feathered bangs.

"They're definitely not for blocking the sun today."

"It's going to be a good day. I'm sure it will be just us, who else is going to be crazy enough to ride in this weather?"

The two headed out to meet the rest of the team in the parking lot and begin the day's 72-mile ride from Mystic to Providence.

Rex stowed his crutches in the support van and collected his bike. He pushed off of the side of the vehicle and ratcheted his pedal up and down turning out of the hotel parking lot onto the thoroughfare with the rest of the group. The freezing drizzle was relentless as the team made its way through traffic, over bridges and finally to the less-busy industrial section of Mystic. It was there, free of guest riders, that the team finally began to gel and come together as a single unit. The camera crew no longer noticeable.

Rex shifted gears, his quadricep welcoming the added tension as he broke out of the paceline and sprinted toward catching up to Kathy.

"OK, Kathy, in ya go." Kathy cut back into the line at the very front as Rex instructed her on the fundamentals of a paceline. "There ya go," encouraged Rex, "now slow up." Kathy stopped pedaling for half a rotation and tapped her brake to slightly reduce her speed. That was all that was required for Rex to easily move in front of her. Rex continued his instruction as he cycled past Kathy, his purple windbreaker puffed out, round, like the Michelin Man. "If you keep your pedal speed

306

up, as you're getting ready to come out of the line, it's a lot easier and faster to cut and make a quick surge."

"OK," Kathy, a bit winded, smiled victoriously as she participated in her first-ever paceline, feeling more able than ever, her neon yellow windbreaker billowing in the wind.

Rex cut in and took the lead allowing Kathy to conserve energy by drafting off his wheel. The paceline lesson was complete. While riding in the lead, working hard against the headwind, crystals formed on his nose hairs. It was hard and miserable and his first physical challenge of the ride. Paul's words from their meeting a few nights earlier played through his mind.

"I know when we talked two months ago, I told you that I didn't think you would lose fitness." Paul confessed that he underestimated the logistics and pace of riding with hand cyclists and the others' disabilities. He just didn't have enough information back then. "Knowing what I now know, I regret to say that I'm going to have to hold you back and you're going to have to be patient." Those words stung, but Rex knew Paul understood how hard that would be having been a competitor himself. That didn't alleviate Rex's concern about losing fitness. "We're here now and this is what we're doing. I need to know you're committed."

Rex went to bed that night satisfied about how he functioned with the group that day and remembered that life was easier when he just did what he was told.

The next morning brought a renewed energy. Rex attributed it to the fact that it was their last day in the states. It was the seventeenth day on the ride and he was anxious to get to Boston, where Sara would be waiting for him.

Besides the anxiousness to get to the hotel, the ride was uneventful. Rex kept his attitude in check and enjoyed the sights of the city. When he turned into the hotel parking lot his heart began to race, Sara was waiving from the valet drop-off area. Her wide smile accentuated up her cheeks, glowing pink from the chilly air.

Rex rode right up beside her "Hey baby," and they embraced like lovers longing to be touched.

***

Rex sat on the shower stool Sara brought with her. He closed his eyes and his head bobbed back and forth as she stood behind him and pressed into his scalp making a circular motion with her fingers. The shampoo suds streaked white down his back and shoulders. He reached for her hand and brought it to his lips, realizing this was the first time in seventeen days that he felt loved.

"Let's order room service, OK?" whispered Sara.

"Sounds good, baby." Rex turned the shower nozzle more toward hot. " Let's stay here a few more minutes."

Before they knew it, it was 8 p.m., time for the team meeting.

"OK, everybody take a seat. I hope you all enjoyed a nice dinner. I for one took a short nap. Well, here we are, already finished with the first leg of our World Ride? Hats off to all of you!" said Paul.

As they sat in the team circle, listening to Paul, Rex stretched his arm across the back of Sara's chair. He looked around the room at the people he would be spending the next six months with. They seemed different now, more familiar. He knew them, unlike when they sat in the circle after the first day when he just knew about them. Their disabilities and the comparisons he had made disappeared, he only saw people, his team. They were just a group of ordinary citizens who had good days and bad days and were going to ride their bikes around the world together.

"We've got a big day tomorrow and we'll need everyone to help." Paul conveyed to the group the amount of organizing and packing was at the point of overwhelming.

"But, look what I've got." Paul held up their flight itinerary. "Leave Boston tomorrow afternoon, April 7, arrive Shannon Ireland the morning of April 8." Paul instructed the team to keep their travel bags with them, so as not to get those items mixed in the with bike boxes and everything else. "We'll meet back here at 9:00 a.m."

Wanting to get back to the room and spend the time with Sara, Rex kept the introductions short. There was no reason to try and develop new relationships in one evening; he preferred to have the time with just Sara.

Rex lay on top of the blankets while Sara pulled the sheet over her. He flipped through the channels and found Seinfeld. "Nothing like a show about nothing to take your mind off things," Sara said.

"I know. I'm going to be gone for a long time." Rex rolled on his side and faced Sara.

"I'm so glad you're getting this opportunity. I want you to enjoy every minute of it." Sara tucked Rex's hair behind his ear.

"Yeah. I hope when we get over there, we'll be able to pick up the pace a little bit."

"Hey, don't worry about that. Your fitness will be fine. Take advantage of this gift. I mean how many people get to ride their bikes around the world?"

"Baby, what did I do to deserve you? Man, I love you."

"I'm going to miss you." Sara grabbed the remote and turned off the television.

Yeah?" Rex scooted closer. "Come here."

33

WORLD RIDE ABROAD PART ONE

Three weeks after the commencing of the ride back in Atlanta, Rex leaned into the airplane wall beside his seat, tilted his head and pressed it against the frame of the window while he gazed out of the small portal to watch the landing. From the sky, Shannon airport looked a lot like Logan airport. Both were surrounded by water, and grass, which looked like large green geometric puzzle pieces fit together with long gray strips of runway crisscrossing through. On the side farthest from the ocean was a cluster of buildings and past that, a multitude of cars. It was beyond the parking lot where the difference was notable. Shannon's population was less than 10,000.

Jet-lagged, he daydreamed of wrapping himself in the grassy knolls, that now closer to the ground, transformed from puzzle pieces into a never-ending blanket crocheted in the richest of greens. There was so much green. As the wheels touched down Rex's forehead bumped against the hard plastic; he rubbed his eyes and sat up.

The pilot began to speak over the intercom. "Welcome to Shannon, Ireland, local time is 7:22 a.m., it's 64 degrees with just a bit of a gust coming off the ocean. Looks like it's going to be a beautiful day. Enjoy your stay and we look forward to flying with you again."

Once off the plane, Rex helped unload, along with the rest of the team, as Paul began orchestrating the daunting chore of unpacking the boxes, reassembling the bicycles, picking up the rental van, packing it with every spare part imaginable, reviewing the map, and meeting with their in-country hosts.

By the time the team took off on their bikes, there were only a few daylight hours left for riding. Rex, anxious to stretch his leg, just wanted to ride hard and feel the sea air on his face. The unobstructed roads begged to be ridden fast. With no guest riders on that first day, Paul let the team ride faster than he had in the congestion of American cities.

As the team pedaled away from the airport, Rex looked out over the river Shannon, beyond its grassy banks, to Bunratty Castle. The tall, weathered, gray stone structure made a statement of time-tested-strength while it's crown-topped towers dominated the sky, demanding the attention of onlookers for miles around.

As days passed, the shrub-lined-single-lanes of Portlaoise and the open planes of Shrewsbury brought a calm to Rex's soul. The slow tense riding stayed back in the states and the villages and canals of Ireland became the backdrop for daily living. The simplicity pulled on Rex as he and the other riders high-fived the street side congregates, who came out to support the riders, and they lifted a hand to the cheers of those standing further back.

In the quaint town of Naas, the group stopped to order chicken filet rolls for lunch. The bikes crowded the one-lane street adorned with pennant streamers swaying overhead, attached to the rooftops. In the colors of the Irish flag, the green, white and orange pennants created a festive atmosphere, counter to the traditional candy cane shaped street lamps. A young boy leaned out the window of a passing car and waived to the riders.

The longer the team rode across Europe, the more people heard of the event and began to join the cause. At any given time, there could be up to thirty guest riders. Some joined the group for a day, others stayed for a month. On the inevitable slower-paced days that came with the additional riders, Rex decided to engage and listen to their stories, rather than obsess about the snail's pace.

A shift took place in his attitude as he stayed focused on the reason he was there; to create awareness. The people who joined in came with a variety of disabilities; the fact that they were there meant the ride was doing what it was supposed to; include everybody.

One evening the group went out to a pub. The dimly lit dark-wooded establishment smelled of savory Shepard's Pie. Rex was looking for Dan, a sandy-haired, joyful Irishman, who joined the group as a guest rider.

"Here, I'm here, lad," said Dan, as he hopped over to Rex on his left leg, through the patrons, who gathered around.

"My left foot. There you are." Rex greeted Dan with widespread arms. "A question I get asked a lot, is 'what do I do with my other shoe'? well, here you go! If we both put them on and took a picture of our feet, no one would know that it's two different people." Laughter rang out across the bar as onlookers raised there pints of beer in solidarity.

"Oh, thank you, my friend." Dan's smile crinkled his eyes almost shut, however, the joy still shone through as he held up the shoe and acknowledged the clapping patrons.

A few days later, Rex found himself enjoying wordless conversations with Bolek, an older Polish man, who spoke no English and was missing both hands and forearms. A tin box, he picked up while walking in a field, exploded in his hands,

Rex riding along side of Bolek, jerked his head when he heard the "zzzzzzzzzzzztttt," noise of Bolek's front tire rubbing the back tire of the cyclist directly in front of him.

Oh shit, the words rang audibly as Rex watched Bolek lose control and skid five feet down the road, his bike twisting and turning. Bolek's knees and elbows scrapped up, bloody and full of gravel from his body bouncing across the pavement. The cyclist that Bolek bumped into was also laying on the ground in a heap.

On one of the twists, Bolek's bicycle hit Rex causing him to lose control of his own wobbling bike. Rex ran over the cyclist and tumbled to the ground himself. He sat, shaken, looking around at the others in the pile-up.

34

WORLD RIDE ABROAD PART TWO

A month had come and gone since the team landed in Ireland. As beautiful and charming as the European towns and villages were, Rex was becoming bored with the monotonous days. The slow pace was again trying his nerves. On May, 27, day 72 of the World Ride, now in Poland, Rex needed to mix things up and decided to ride one of the hand cycles.

"No, no," directed Rex, to a teammate who wanted to push the back of the hand cycle chair to help Rex climb a steep hill.

"OK, sorry man. I just knew it was your first time riding a hand cycle." The teammate let go.

"Yeah, it's kicking my ass. I can do it, I don't want any help," replied Rex, veins popped from his burning biceps.

On the way down the hill, Rex loosened his grasp on the hand cycle grips and spread apart his fingers to relax his stiff hands. It was a beautiful ride from Krakow to Kielce, Poland. His chest expanded as he filled his lungs. The azure sky outlined the plush emerald landscape across the horizon. Short brick walls bordered acres of land holding in thick-coated sheep that dotted the hills and meadows.

By simply altering the daily grind of slow-paced riding, Rex felt a new rhythm to the day. The extra focus also helped him to rid the sadness that penetrated him after riding past Ghetto Heroes Square and seeing the long row of bronze chairs lined across the gray cobblestone. He briefly struggled with his old mindset wanting to immediately identify with the victims shot down by the Nazi soldiers. That self-pity mentality was still a daily thorn in his side. The inherent tension of it crept up and begun to affect the group again. Fellow World Riders kept their distance from Rex when his talk became negative. Before it ramped to that point on this day, a shift took place and without trying the battling voices in his head went quiet and his body sat taller, like he was garnering strength from the survivors of the Holocaust, from the people who never gave up. He rode the hand-cycle the whole way; sixty-eight miles.

Five days later, Rex and his team crossed into Russia at Brest, Belarus. The charming villages of the past thirty days gave way to farms where hefty women wearing Quaker style dresses drove horse and plows. Gone were the fragrant shrub-lined streets. They had turned into long stretches of potholed pavement through brown fields. It was as if time stood still compared to the cosmopolitan city of Boston. As the view became less and less interesting to look at and the street conditions worsened, so did Rex's attitude at a time when team cohesiveness was very important. Diplomacy with Russia was tense and the World Ride leaders feared that a rift in the team could cause unwanted attention to the gang.

Four armed escorts joined the group for protection. They soon became just another part of the team. When there were no hotels everyone slept in tents along the side of the road. The flavorful food of the European countries was now just a memory, having been replaced by bland and unsatisfying meals of kasha and cabbage. The Russian people, however, were friendly, and proud to have their country be a part of the World Ride cause.

After four weeks of being in Russia, on the day the team was nearing their stop in Zlatoust, it began to rain. Paul, the team captain, told the drivers to pull over and directed the team to get into the vans, it was becoming too dangerous to continue on the bicycles. Everyone except Rex piled in.

"I'll see you at the hotel, I'm going to keep riding," Rex said to Kathy, the able-bodied rider

"If that's your choice. Be careful, man."

Rex felt the warm sprinkles on the back of his neck and could see tiny bubbles as they landed on his hands. *It's only thirty miles, this is nothing,* he thought as he rode down the rugged street steering around the cows in the middle of the rode.

As the occasional economy car passed by, the headlights were blurry in the rain and spotlighted the large drops now coming down like crystal ropes. The sky turned darker and streaks of lightning were easily visible as they flashed across the sky. Now and then an onlooker would wave from the porch of their small wooden home. *I'm not a quitter* he told himself as he turned into the motel parking lot. The yellow and white concrete building with large windows and balconies looked very modern compared to the street he just rode down.

"Why didn't you get in the Van?" Paul met Rex in the parking lot when he rode up.

"I didn't think the storm was bad enough for me to stop riding." Rex removed his helmet and shook the rain off of it.

"That's not the point, Rex."

"I'm sorry, I came here to ride."

"I made a judgment call and asked you to get in the van. It was a matter of safety."

"I came here to ride, not get in the van. I came to ride every mile," Rex said, with no remorse.

"Make sure you're at the meeting tonight." Paul walked away.

Rex stowed his bike and retrieved his crutches from the van. He walked through the small parking lot that was overrun with white extra-long vans covered in sponsor decals and rooftop bike racks loaded with bicycles. He could feel the stares of his teammates as he walked by those milling about the lobby, nobody spoke to him. It was the same when he entered the meeting room.

"I was not aware of the fact that Rex didn't get into a van at the time I asked everyone to do so." Paul spoke to the team. "I was told after we started driving that he kept riding. Safety and compliance are serious issues in any foreign country and especially Russia. We're here as their guests and we need to act accordingly. So this predicament is going to be addressed. Rex?"

"As I said in the parking lot, I didn't believe the rain was heavy enough to stop riding." Rex adjusted the strap on his Teva sandal. "I came here to ride every mile."

Paul continued to address Rex about his lack of following direction, bad attitude and commitment. "Rex, aside from the obstacles we have not been able to resolve, my biggest concern is; I'm not sure you even want to be here."

"I'm as committed to this ride as anybody, but I'm not going to go against what I stand for, which is giving it my all every single time."

"Well, you have the choice to be more compliant or if you feel like you should go home, maybe that's what needs to be done."

"If staying means I have to sell out, no, I can't stay." Rex already acquiesced to riding at a slow pace; he was not willing to ease up on his commitment to ride every mile just to please the corporate authorities.

The next day, July 2, 108 days into the ride, Rex hugged his teammates' goodbye and was taken to the airport. He used the time sitting in the terminal to reflect on what transpired; he couldn't make sense of it. Was it his deep-rooted trouble with authority figures that made him negative? Was he still so self-centered that he couldn't just do what he was told, knowing that things always work out better that way? Why did he think getting in the van would be selling out? He wanted to complete the World Ride. He hated the idea of quitting. He simply couldn't risk not being ready for the Paralympics, even though it was still a year away. If he wanted a spot on the podium, it was required he be in top shape physically and mentally. He needed to think like the elite athlete he was and do whatever it took to win – including leaving the World Ride early.

He thought of both scenarios and checked his body. While pondering the World Ride, his body tightened and when he imagined the Paralympics he felt energized. Sure about his gratitude toward the World Ride, he decided to move forward, *I'm a thoroughbred, being chained to a cart doesn't work for me.*

On the flight home, strong in the attitude of what's next, Rex thought about his future. Not just the upcoming Paralympics, but also his life with Sara. They had been together for over two-years, and their oppositeness blended perfectly. It was time to take the next step in their relationship as well.

Once home, he bought a ring. On New Year's Day 1996, Rex packed a picnic and took Sara to their favorite scenic view overlooking Denver. Rex faced Sara and retrieved a small box from his jeans pocket. "Baby, will you marry me?"

"You know I will," Sara answered with no hesitation.

"Let's get married after the Atlanta Games, at the campground."

"How about September, a fall wedding?

35

ATLANTA

On August 16, 1996, along with 3,500 athletes, representing 127 nations, Rex marched onto the field of Centennial Olympic Stadium, the World Ride now a distant memory. Swelled with pride of country and the sense of wonderment from knowing he was a part of something much bigger than himself, he looked at all the flags arching around the upper deck like a global rainbow and at Jose Alcala, his Paralympic coach, who was also grinning ear to ear, and shook his head. He had no words to describe the moment. Feeling as if he was being carried around the track by the thunderous applause booming from the 66,000 spectators, Rex closed his eyes hard, but the arena was still blurry when he opened them as supporters waving their countries' flags blended from one nation to the next, like an impressionistic painting.

This was the first Paralympic Games to attract mass media since its inception in 1800. The disabled community was becoming more accepted into the mainstream and, as with women athletes and some other sports, gaining a new appreciation from sporting organizations and fans. Rex was a part of this history-making event, which was living up to its motto, *Triumph of the Human Spirit*. The mascot, Blaze, was a cartoon depiction of a Phoenix; a mythical eagle-like bird representing destruction and rebirth. It featured a royal blue body and wings, its feet dancing candle flames and neon green feathers hung low on its chest like a ruffled collar. The bird's chin tilted up, as it looked toward the left wing, held high, a flame coming out of its hand, similar to the fire swaying from atop the Cauldron. The right wing tucked down by its side. It captured the essence of those athletes who at some point felt that a part of them had been destroyed, then rose from the ashes like a phoenix.

As powerful as the moment was, after the American cycling team was introduced, Rex left the opening ceremony; there was one thing more important – winning.

He walked back to his room, passing the frolicking water fountains and towering light columns shaped like giant baseball bats illuminating the night sky. His room was plain – just enough essentials to be comfortable.

"How was it?" asked his roommate, Bob, who was sitting on the couch watching the show on television.

"It was cool, there was a lot of energy in that stadium," answered Rex, (who almost didn't go due to his early morning start.) "I came here to win, not listen to speeches. My Road Race is early, I'm going to get my stuff ready then hit the hay."

"I hear ya, my race is early, too."

Rex lay in his bed visualizing his race, a soft glow peeping under the door from the hall light. He regulated his breathing, inhale 2,3,4, he counted as his stomach rose and fell with each breath of 4 counts. He moved up his body starting from his toes and released the tension from all of his muscles. The low-toned buzzing from cars on the highway lulled him into a deeper relaxation. In his mind, he inspected every gear and heard the click as he shifted up and down. He felt his foot clamp into the pedal and pictured his leg moving in a circular motion the words *you've already won, you just have to ride the race* scrolled in front of his closed eyes, like on a teleprompter. The next thing he knew it was time to get up and catch the bus.

"Good morning," Rex said to Andy Pruit, his mentor and team physician, who was stationed near the starting line.

"Good morning to you. How are you?" asked Andy.

"I feel good. I slept a lot. I'm a little nervous; you know, I've done this hundreds of times, but there's nothing like the Games."

"I know what you mean. Be smart, you're favored to win."

When the announcer called out for the competitors to make their way to the starting line, Rex pulled up alongside his teammate, Pier, and their eyes met. An inaudible conversation took place, *this is it for us, we're old and probably won't be doing this again.* The announcer began to count down.

"Good luck," Pier extended his hand.

"Good luck, man," Rex gave one firm, quick shake of his hand.

The gun sounded, and Rex began to ratchet. It wasn't long before the thirteen riders were spread out into a paceline formation. *This Road Race is long, be smart, pace yourself.* Rex began his self-talk to keep from exerting too much energy too soon. That had cost him in the past and he wasn't going to let that happen now.

In the cool, grey-skied morning, Rex reached around and pulled down the back of his jersey where it bunched up. It was red around the bottom and white across the chest and shoulders with a wide blue stripe down the middle. Red stars looked as if they were fizzling up from mid-torso.

By an hour into the race, he pedaled his way to a contending position, feeling relaxed and strong of mind. Then everything changed. He shifted gears and threw his chain. Heart pounding, he pulled over and hopped off.

His grease-covered fingertips shook as link by link Rex placed the chain back on the sprocket. The hum of spokes whirring by closed in on him and made it hard to concentrate. One competitor after another sped by, causing a bigger and bigger lump to form in his throat.

"Come on fucker," Rex yelled, fighting back rage as he noticed no more bikes were passing by.

As the last link finally slipped into place, he rolled to his right side and pushed up with his hands in the void space of his left leg and popped up, butt first. In two small hops, he was in position standing next to his bike and slid his left butt cheek onto the seat. Pushing off with his right foot, like on a skateboard, he got back in the race.

Shaken, he was now overthinking everything. *There's still time, it's a long race, you're OK, you'll be in a good position again... relax.* His thumping heart slowed down as one by one he caught up to and flew by his competitors.

Perspiration stung his eyes as he turned his head and glanced behind. He regained the lead position.

Poised to win again, he regulated his breathing and relaxed his body into a steady pace. Twenty minutes later his chain dislodged for the second time and by then it was too late to regain a front position.

With a time of 1:46:39, he came in ninth. His teammate, Pier Beltrami, right behind him, was tenth. At the staging area, Rex threw his bike down, grabbed his crutches and stormed off. He saw Andy looking at him from a distance, but just kept walking. Andy knew to leave him alone. One of Rex's only two chances at bringing home a medal was gone.

Completely deflated, Rex fell into Sara's arms at the staging area, where she had been waiting. "Come on, let's get my stuff. I want to go home."

"Baby, I'm not taking you home. You actually think I would take you home?" Sara knew how much this meant to Rex.

"Yeah, I want to get out of here. It's not worth it." Rex squeezed Sara tighter.

"Listen to what you are saying. Where is the Rex that never quits?"

"I don't care, I'm done." Rex's voice quivered.

"How about this? Stick it out for one more day and if tomorrow you still want to leave, I'll take you home."

"I know what you're doing, miss psychologist" Rex let go of his hug and wiped his eyes.

"Good! Now fix that stupid chain, get back on your bike and shake it off. You have a few days before your next race."

Rex took some time for himself and rode around Centennial Park that afternoon. He stopped at the area where the pipe bomb exploded while Jack Mack and the Heart Attack was performing a free concert, during the regular 1996 Olympics. The bomb, hidden inside a backpack was left on the ground, the blast caused by the crude device killed one person and injured 112 others. Pondering the victims' misfortune, Rex sat on a bench for a long time wrestling with his own loss, not his leg, the race. He knew logically the two incidents were nowhere near the same, it was only his ego that got hurt. Still, he was struggling with making peace with his disappointment. He called Andy.

"Rex, you've won titles and medals all along the way," said Andy, likening Rex's accomplishments to refueling stations on his ascension to Atlanta. "With each stop you became more respected, more validated, and you served as a force that caused your sport to be regarded more seriously. Rex, you've worked hard for yourself and disabled cycling. There will always be disappointments. This one doesn't erase what you have already accomplished."

"Thanks for the pep talk. This morning I asked Sara to take me home."

"Don't be ridiculous. Take these few days to get your head straight for your next race. Call me later."

Rex put his phone in his pouch and went over to another athlete who was also somberly milling around the area.

"We all have our demons," said Rex

"That we do," replied the tall, thin man with an African accent.

"But, that bombing was pretty fucked up."

"Indeed it was, hurt a lot of innocent people."

Rex nodded as the man turned to walk away.

"Good luck in your event," the man said and continued.

At dusk, Rex sat on a bench and breathed in the thick air. Kids were playing in the fountains shaped like the Olympic rings. He smiled as they laughed and danced around with the water as it changed colors each time it shot up from the ground. A little further down was the torch, now glowing in the night sky. The cauldron sat atop a tall metal structure that looked like scaffolding, the long silver bars crisscrossing their way up the 21-story tower.

The flame was wide, more like a bonfire on the beach than the flame of a candle. *It doesn't look like a torch.* The red and blue cauldron shined against the contrast of the yellow flames. Rex stared at it for a long time trying to figure out what it reminded him of. *It's the shape of a French fries box and the fire looks like the French fries. No wonder I'm getting hungry.*

***

"The track is still too wet," said the official. Rex and the others groaned upon hearing that news.

"We'll wait for another hour and check again. If it's not dry enough to race by then, we'll have to cancel today's events."

"What! We've all ridden in worse than this," said Rex, but not loud enough for the official to hear him.

"It's stopped raining and the sun is coming out, the track will be safe in an hour. Don't worry about it," Jose consoled Rex.

"I'm just here to race, man."

"We all are, relax." Jose not letting Rex fall into a pity party.

Rex stepped out from beneath the overhang. Clouds moved across the sky casting an alternating pattern of shadow and sunshine over the velodrome. The sun beat hot when it wasn't blocked by clouds. He pulled the sunscreen from the pouch fastened to his crutches and rubbed it on his neck. *Why can't we just start?*

Rex traipsed about the stadium as he waited for the all clear to begin the Omnium, an individual multi-stage event in which the competitor races solo against the clock and points are awarded after each stage depending on the athlete's time.

"Hey Rex let's go, the officials just announced we can start the race," Jose yelled. Rex hustled over to the staging area, taking such long strides with his crutches that it seemed like he was about to pole vault.

There was another time trial before his, so he and Jose had a time to get ready, but not much. The race would take less than seven minutes.

The gun sounded. Fighting the urge to watch the clock, Jose quickly brought Rex's bike over. As soon as Jose stopped in front of Rex, he grasped the seat and gave it a firm shake – it broke.

"What the fuck?" Rex met Jose's eyes and saw panic.

Everything he worked so hard for, flashed across his mind.

"Oh, shit," answered Jose.

"Is there another seat?" Rex's mind racing. *How can this be happening?*

"No, we didn't bring one. How long has it been since you changed the seat?"

"A long time. We have to find another one and we need to find it now."

"Fuck!" Jose felt the pressure.

The coach for England's team overheard their predicament.

"Hey Rex, I have a seat you can use." He ran the seat to Jose, who removed the broken one.

"Thanks, man." Rex and Jose, appreciative.

Rex glanced at the clock, 4:08:731, while Jose hurried to secure the seat and clumsily dropped his wrench.

"Shit! Rex, I'm not going to be able to fine tune the adjustments, there's just not enough time." Jose anxious knowing he would not be able to get the seat to the correct degree of tilt, or exactly how high up from the frame the seat should sit or how far back the seat needs to be from the handlebars to be optimum placement for Rex's body.

Rex looked again, 4:22: 391, panic welled up through his nerve endings. "Screw it, just get the seat on."

"I'm giving it my best guess. All those years of figuring out the precise adjustments of your saddle and it comes down to just slapping the damn thing on for the biggest race of your life."

With seconds to spare, Jose tightened the last bolt and they hustled to the starting line. Rex locked his right foot into the pedal clamp as the bike holder held up his light blue Bianchi

Fixie, a single speed, fixed gear bicycle with no brakes. Sitting upright on the ill-fitted saddle he shifted his butt back and forth; there was no comfortable spot. He cinched tight the nylon chinstrap on his blue and black Pearl Izumi helmet and pulled up his short-fingered matching cycling gloves. He bent over and clasped the end of the handlebars and fiddled with his fingers until they settled into the worn-down grooves, then squeezed, not too tight. He put his head down and prayed.

It was the 4 Kilometer Standing Start Time Trial. He could barely stifle the anger pent up inside, but understood how to make that energy work for him, and planned to expend it wisely during the almost 2.5-mile race. The horn blew, the bike holder let go, and Rex began to ratchet his pedal up and down harder than he ever had before. His upper body bore down on the handlebars to keep the front wheel from lifting off the steep, wooden, oval track. In two seconds, he made a full pedal rotation, increasing speed and momentum with each lap until he reached the pace he trained for. He flew around the track as though his bike were turbocharged, his piston thigh pushing down and pulling up. His arms bending and raising with each pedal stroke, triceps burning. His brow furrowed with intensity, and sweat soaked the back of his jersey. Then, when it was time, he put the hammer down and exploded through his last two laps.

As Rex crossed the finish line, Jose bolted toward him.

"We won, we won!" Jose waving his arms wildly.

Rex looked at Jose and gestured his right arm to the side, not hearing Jose. He circled the track again, to slow down.

"We won, we won!" Jose jumping up and down and running toward Rex.

"We won?" asked Rex, still too deep in his mental zone to fully understand what was going on.

"Check the clock, you set a world record!" Jose jogging at his side, helping to bring his bike to a complete stop.

Rex oriented himself and found the jumbo timekeeper. 5.59.816. He averaged twenty-two seconds a lap for the sixteen lap Time Trial, finishing at less than a second under six minutes.

Rex dropped his head in a combination of disbelief and humility, beads of sweat dripped off the end of his nose. After a few seconds, he whispered, "I did it."

36

AFTER ATLANTA

While pouring himself a cup of coffee, Rex heard the sounds of familiar voices chatting behind him. It was good to be home – at his Tuesday night Fellowship. The dingy plastic chairs he sat uncomfortably in almost every week for several years were inviting, he was excited to be there. He sucked on his stir stick then tossed it in the small trash can underneath the beverage table. He didn't see Bobby come in.

"Hey it's the man of the hour," Bobby yelled from across the room.

"And it's the man with the loud voice honoring us with his presence." Rex still had his back to Bobby.

"Get over here, man." Bobby gave Rex a bear hug.

The meeting was called to order and Rex and Bobby took seats next to each other in the large circle of folding chairs. In each chair sat a comrade who was eager to hear Rex share. After the 12-Steps were read, the leader asked who wanted to go first.

"I'll go. Hi, I'm Rex, drug addict."

"Hi, Rex." The whole group replied together.

"About seven years ago, I rediscovered this thing called a bicycle and on the day that happened something woke up inside of me. Almost five years ago you all helped me fulfill a dream and raised funds for me to go to the Paralympic Games in Barcelona. I was ashamed because I didn't win a medal, but a wise man reminded me that I was eighth in the world. I kept training, got better and as most of you know, I just got back from Atlanta."

Rex made eye contact with each person in the circle, their eyes glued on him. A little uncomfortable from the acute attention, he fiddled with his hat, retrieved the silver medal from his pouch and held it up.

"This time I came home with this. It's not just mine, it's ours. Without you, I wouldn't have it. So, thank you for believing in that fat, toothless, crippled guy who crawled into this room all those years ago without a shred of hope. I love you, you're my family."

"We love you too, Rex."

"You the man!" came shouts from the group of people from all walks of life.

After the meeting Rex and Bobby hung out in the parking lot for a while, Bobby continued doting over Rex for being a hometown hero.

"OK, OK, I appreciate it man, that's enough. There is one more thing, Rex added, I got a call today and was invited to speak at a school assembly in two weeks."

"Of course you did, the world is yours, my man, my hometown hero."

Rex arrived early at the neighborhood high school and sat in his truck going over his notes. He spoke at numerous NA meetings and some NA conventions, but never in front of children. Sara approved his speech the night he rehearsed it in their living room. He trusted her and felt prepared, except for the nervousness that comes with being in front of a live audience and knowing things might not go as planned.

He was greeted in the school lobby by the principal, who helped him with his bike and got him set up off to the side in the multipurpose room. Hearing all of the commotion as the students came in, Rex peeked around the curtain. There were so many kids and teachers -- *please just don't say fuck.*

The principal settled the fidgety crowd and introduced Rex. When he heard his name, Rex rode his bike to the podium at the front of the stage, right leg toward the audience. He appeared normal. Everyone was clapping. He stopped behind the podium where his crutches had been stored. When he stepped to the side and his body came into full view, there was a gasp, then the room went silent.

"This medal is from the Paralympic games, in Atlanta, where I competed in August," Rex began his speech.

He went on to tell the students that the medal marked the pinnacle of a hardfought climb, a rise that encompassed so much more than cycling. He conveyed to the kids that he recognized that his success offers possibility and inspiration to people still being sidelined by a self-defeating belief system and personally, his high achievement was redemption for that little kid who grew up in Arkansas and for so many years wanted to float away.

"That young boy is now me and people say that I have become a role model for kids coming up behind me, children who wish they, too, could disappear."

Not a sound was made while Rex was speaking. He knew he held their full attention and was empowered as he walked back and forth across the stage, pleased at how smoothly his words were coming out.

"I made some bad choices and you can see the result. So, I want to leave you with this: Next time you are on the verge of making a bad choice, doing something stupid, ask yourself – is it going to be worth it? Is it worth what could happen to me, what could happen to my family and the people who love me, what it could put them through? And, most importantly, answer honestly. I've overcome my obstacles and so can you. Thanks for listening."

The audience erupted in applause, the Principal came back out, and Rex, relieved, didn't have to stand there alone feeling awkward, not knowing if he was supposed to exit. "What did you think of Rex?" Cheers became louder when the Principal asked the audience. "Rex, your testimony will not easily be forgotten. The physical evidence of your mistakes is powerful, as is your victory over them when you held up your medals. Thanks for talking to our students."

Pleased with himself, Rex heaved his bike over the side of his truck bed next to the open driver's side door, which he used for balance, then hopped in. As soon as the engine started, the radio came on loud. Instead of singing along, Rex turned it off, wanting to be with his thoughts. He rolled down the window and breathed deep as the autumn crispness brushed across his face; he shivered.

During his introspection, he discovered that so far, 1996 had been the best year of his life. He went to new levels in his athletic ability, reached deeper places spiritually, felt emotionally grounded, and he would soon be marrying Sara. He reveled in the good news and resisted the urge to add a *but*. He pulled to the side of the road when tears so flooded his eyes he could no longer see. He was completely overwhelmed with gratitude

37

MARRIAGE

Rex stepped out of his cabin and one more time checked to make sure his left pant leg was tucked securely inside his navy blue trousers. It was September 22, 1996, a day that 36-year-old Rex was convinced would never eventuate. A day that had died and crumbled, like the brown brittle leaves swirling about the dirt pathway. He thought about the defiant little boy who grew up believing he was unlovable and so found what he was looking for, as empty as it was, through drugs and prostitutes. His accident compounded that belief, because who would want a cripple.

Settled, at the altar next to his best man, he felt alive, vibrant and connected to his surroundings. To this opening in the woods, that was filled with love, light and friends. It was an event Rex wanted everyone to know about. The opposite of a time twenty-five-years prior in another opening in the woods, where he was left for trash on a dark, hopeless, lonely night, wishing to die.

Now, his past was almost unrecognizable. Rex did the hard work of the twelve-steps and learned new mindsets, which together lead him straight to this moment. Of all the significant days he chalked up; his last first day of sobriety, getting his GED, winning a silver medal at the Paralympics, this day above all felt like a resurrection - *things that were dead really can come back to life.* As much as this was for Rex the man, it was also for Rex the child.

A cool autumn breeze refreshed the guests as they stood up from their folding chairs in a small field at Rex's favorite campground. The bride was approaching the modest setting. Two-foot logs standing upright capped the end of each row of seats. Atop the logs were arrangements of pink and white carnations in baskets resembling straw hats. The flowers added a pop of color against the shades of green and yellow that painted the forest backdrop, as the foliage turned colors.

Sara looked angelic in her simple, flowy white gown and baby breath tiara. Her rosy cheeks radiant, her smile gleaming. Enraptured, Rex watched his beloved come towards him.

Long gone are the days of Rex wanting to float away into a drug-induced stupor. It was only two years ago that he experienced this new, better, kind of floating – falling in love – and now his bride appeared to be floating towards him as guests cheered and snapped photos of Sara making her way down the aisle toward her man.

Their ardent vows expressed the hard work of vulnerability each put into the relationship and how deep love was birthed from that intrepidity.

As Rex and Sara blended their lives more completely, full-time living together soon produced a routine of working at the Community Center, Rex's training, Saturday barbecues and unconditional support of each other's dreams. Sara was working toward her own counseling practice and Rex continued to go after his cycling career. A topic not mentioned when discussing the future, was that of children. They decided to not pursue a life with kids. Working with teenagers at the Center would be their special way to help shape lives of the next generation.

***

In the spring of 1997, Rex competed in the Paralympic Kilometer Time Trial in Colorado Springs and scored another world record in the 200m Time Trial Flying Start, coming in at 13.882 seconds, and received a gold medal. In 1998, he won a road race at the CSUSA competition. He was awarded his final gold medal.

After the CSUSA event, Rex significantly decreased his training efforts and the number of competitions he raced in. He was thirty-seven years old and his body was depleted. Recovery time after a race went from one day to two days and longer. When it became a five day recovery time, Rex and Sara were concerned. This exhaustion was different, it was puzzling – he could not shake it with respite and vitamins. Something else was going on with his health that he was no longer able to ignore. It was time to see a doctor.

"Rex, your test results show that you have Hepatitis C." His doctor delivered the news.

"Doc, you're kidding, right? How can that be?"

"At some point during your drug-using years, you unknowingly became infected with the virus." The doctor explained that the diagnosis of Hepatitis C is rarely made during the acute phase of the disease when a person first comes in contact. The majority of those afflicted experience no symptoms during this phase. Most think they have the flu.

It had been at least a decade since he became infected, and only now the symptoms of his liver damage become noticeable enough for him to think it was something other than the general fatigue owing to hard physical training.

"I'm going to put you on a plan of 48 weekly Interferon injections. It's not chemo, however, the side effects are sometimes the same." The doctor gave Rex a prescription.

"Please tell me that this isn't happening." Rex, slumped, like he had been sucker punched in the gut.

Leaning against the exam table, he stared at the piece of paper in his hand. He crumpled it and started to throw it on the floor, *this is bullshit!* But, he didn't. Straightening out the paper, he rubbed it back and forth across his thigh to uncrinkle it. He couldn't read the scribble, although knew what it said; Interferon injections/4, 12 refills. He put it in his pouch and scheduled his next appointment, his spirit heavy as he walked out the door.

At home, Rex sat on the edge of the bathtub panicked. Starring at the 1cc needle, medicine vile and alcohol swab lined up on the vanity, his heart started to palpitate. The tiny plunger had once controlled his every thought and ruined his life. Now, it was supposed to save it. It was too immense a leap for Rex to reconcile. He reached to pick up the needle, then quickly pulled back his quivering hand.

Too many dark visions seized him. The drug houses, prostitutes, Triangle Park all came back to him in technicolor. He shook his head violently trying to throw them out of his mind. How could such dark times be so colorful? Nothing was making sense. He slid off of the tub and curled up on the floor and in his anguish, cried out to God.

You got me through so many races and the brutal training and have helped keep me sober for all these years....I need you!

His plea went out into the atmosphere and hung there. A weird sensation came over him, almost like a hug or being wrapped in a soft blanket. His heartbeat slowed down and he caught his breath.

Wiping the tears from his eyes, he sat back up and with a steady hand opened the alcohol packet and cleaned the surface on the side of his stomach. He popped the plastic cap off of the needle and inserted the sharp end into the vile tilted it up and slowly pulled back on the plunger, and watched the syringe fill with fluid, careful not to get any air bubbles. His technique was ingrained into his muscle memory, still. He squeezed the fat on his belly to pooch out his skin and injected the needle with one

349

swift poke. Then he waited; nothing ensued. *It's proteins, of course I'm not going to get high.* Spent, he went to bed.

Twenty-four-hours later Rex found himself on the bathroom floor again after heaving his guts. He swished the water around in his mouth and spit it out. He wiped his lips on the hand towel and tried to get the awful noise out of his head. It wasn't long before throwing up became a norm, but the sound was always repulsive.

He decided not to label his day based on whether or not he got sick. It was hard enough to fight the debilitating depression that sidelined him more than he wanted to admit. After he threw-up, he went to the garage to get his clothes out of the dryer and stared at his road bike parked next to it. He swiped his finger along the crossbar and wiped some dust off of the metal. Never before had his bike gone unridden for so long. He felt a twinge in his heart as he bent down and pushed the clothes into the basket placed in front of the dryer door. He couldn't wallow in self-pity, it was time to leave. He was going to work, then out on his mountain bike for as long as his body would hold up.

The Community Center always gave him something to look forward to and take the focus off of himself. However, it was on the trails of the front-range where he reclaimed his peace and felt normal. The nausea and irritability magically disappeared and depression could not taunt him when he was alone with his bike, nature and God. He would toss his head back and rejoice in the sting of the sun burning his cheeks, and the time out of the house. Still, something inside of him shifted; an old door cracked open and the demons flooded in.

Halfway through the year his fight was getting weak. He dealt with the nausea and depression since the beginning, but the prolonged usage of Interferon, and loss of competing, affected his mood. He was irritable all the time and could not overcome the profound sense of malaise that followed him, relentlessly. As time went on, his depression worsened and his thinking became irrational. Stuck in his vortex of misery, he pushed Sara away from emotional intimacy and accused her of not being supportive. Using the excuse of not feeling well, he denied her advances, and accused her of not being physically attracted to him. He was sabotaging their marriage and what once was a carefree relationship now became another thing to dread. By the end of 1999, his marriage to Sara dissolved.

38

THAILAND

More than eight years had passed Since Rex's last competition. During those years he found a new normal living an ordinary life of work, recreational riding, on the road and mountains, his NA meetings and motivational speaking. His rosy cheeks and bright smile hid the discontentment that plagued him since his bout with Hepatitis C.

After Rex's divorce from Sara, he was in and out of relationships, each becoming more unhealthy than the last. He managed to stay clean and sober from drugs and alcohol, although a strong urge to get away by himself dominated his thoughts. One morning before work Rex met with Bobby at a local coffee shop. Rex shared his plans to go to Thailand. "I just want to ride an elephant in the jungle and visit some Temples. It will be a great place to clear my head." Rex wanted to get away by himself and regain some of the confidence that competing gave him, but had dwindled over the past few years.

Bobby didn't like the idea of Rex going alone, and thought he was asking for trouble. Not taking an accountability partner was a bad idea.

Rex understood his friend's concerns about traveling alone. He did his best to persuade Bobby that there is nothing to worry about. "I love you, man. I appreciate you watching out for me. I gotta go." Rex patted Bobby on the back as he got up to leave.

Rex buckled his seatbelt, then sat for a minute in the cab of his truck. There was a peculiar sensation, like somebody was watching him. He shivered as a strange presence permeated the area. He looked around, there was nothing out-of-the-ordinary. Dismissing the aberrant moment, he went to work. On his way home, Rex stopped at the travel agent and booked a month-long trip to Thailand.

Rex told the travel agent his wishes. "I want to be able to take day trips to the jungle, riding an elephant is a must. I also want to be able to go to Bangkok, and see some temples while I'm there,"

"OK, let's find you a nice place on the peninsula midway between Bangkok and the Elephant reserve, there are temples everywhere, so that won't be a problem."

With his tickets in hand, Rex drove home already feeling like a new man. His hands tapped the steering wheel to the rhythm of Doc Watson's, "Walk on Boy." As he belted out the bluegrass tune, a weight lifted at the thought of escaping his life for a little while. But, upon pulling into his driveway, that eerie impression of someone watching him returned; he looked around before getting out of the truck and again nothing was there.

The two weeks since booking his vacation dragged on. Finally, the day arrived. Rex zipped up his suitcase and made his final X on the calendar just before Bobby knocked on the door.

"Taxi service right on time!" Bobby smiled as Rex opened the door.

"I'm ready, right on time!" Rex picked up his bag.

"I don't want to lecture you, man, I just want you to be careful while you're in Thailand. A lot of people have your back on this end, but there's nobody over there." Rex listened as, again, Bobby made his concerns known on the drive to the airport.

"I hear you. I appreciate it, man. I'm good, I'm OK. You don't need to worry."

"Well, you know my phone is always on."

"As many times as you have already talked me off the ledge, I won't be shy. I'll call if I'm in trouble."

***

The rain made the thick air smell sweet as Rex programmed the GPS on top of the dashboard in his rental car. He paid close attention to the directions. After traveling for almost twenty hours he did not want to get lost. Gray to black billowing clouds filled the sky as he drove for an hour to his hotel. Intermittent showers poured down and the sun shone through where the clouds were separated. A full rainbow spanned the horizon. The tension drained out of Rex's body as he thought about spending a whole month in this tropical paradise.

His modest hotel offered a continental breakfast, which he planned to never be awake for, excluding days when he wanted early morning walks on the beach, two blocks away. There were plenty of restaurants to choose from when he felt like getting up. The touristy area accommodated anything a visitor might be interested in, including a bustling nightlife.

Rex woke up from his first-day jet lag, just as the sun was going down. He showered and went to find something to eat. Lights crammed the streets, but not like in New York. Here, the lights were low, and concentrated. They ran together making it hard to tell one establishment apart from another. Before he became too overwhelmed by all the stimulation in this foreign country, he went into the next restaurant and sat down. The waitress came over and filled a glass of water, then took her note pad and pen out of her apron pocket. Rex pointed at number 7. The picture resembled some kind of curry soup.

Still jet lagged, after dinner he went back to his room for the night. He sat on the edge of the bed and leaned his crutches against the wall. He turned the television on and flipped through a bunch of channels before landing on a local station running a show about the rainforests. After watching the show for a few minutes, he turned off the light on the bedside dresser. Immediately upon the room becoming dark, except for the television, that sinister sense of someone peering at him emanated, causing him to sit up.

Being in an unfamiliar place and the acuteness of the feeling caused by the intensity of the energy, Rex turned the light back on and looked around.

"This is stupid. I don't know what the fuck or who the fuck has been following me around lately, but get the hell out of here right now," Rex said out loud, talking as if there were a ghost in the room.

Sighing he turned the light back off, lay down and continued watching about ecosystems of the jungle, confident he was alone,

On his third day there, Rex went on a tour. The small bus drove down dirt roads flanked by the gnarled trunks of Lianes trees. The twisting leaf-filled branches arched high above the bus forming a magnificent emerald canopy over the trails as they drove through the rainforest to the elephant reserve.

The water felt cool as the elephant Rex was riding dipped into the river flowing through the Chiang Mai mountains. He slipped off of the elephant and waded in the cove as his companion for the day raised her trunk and sprayed water into Rex's face.

"Hey, what are you doing"? Rex said, splashing water back at Nica. Her large floppy ears waving back and forth.

Rex floated on his back in complete peace, listening to the buzzing of the jungle and observing the plethora of greens that surrounded him. The sun shone on the lush landscape to his right and made the jade tones brighter. The conversation of the guides contradicted the environment as their nasal voices rose above the nature sounds. He didn't know what they were saying, but they were laughing, so it didn't bother him. There hadn't been enough laughter in his life lately.

When the excursion was over, Rex plopped onto the buses seat cushions, tired from the all-day adventure. It was only minutes before the ride lulled him to sleep for the hour-and-a-half trip back to his hotel. The sound of the air brake releasing woke Rex up from his deep slumber. Disoriented, he looked out the window to see that he was already back at his hotel.

"Thank you," Rex inserted a couple of dollars into the driver's tip container and saw that it was nine o'clock, as he exited the bus.

He quickly showered then walked to his favorite restaurant, the one he went to his first night.

"Hello, good to see you again. Right this way" said the hostess in broken English recognizing Rex when he walked in.

The small eatery was warmly lit with a candle at each of the tables. The two young girls he talked with the last time were there. He waved. They waved back, picked up their drinks and walked over to his table.

"Hi Rex," they said in unison.

"You remember my name, that's good," Rex covered his mouth as he yawned.

"Yes, do you remember mine?" asked the taller of the two. Her bright red lipstick left an impression of her lips on the rim of her beer glass.

"Trisha right?"

"I'm Trisha, she's Vicki," said the more petite one, whom Rex could barely understand. Her bright pink blouse matched the blush on her cheeks. Her black hair fell to her waist.

"We're a lot of fun," said Trisha, as she sipped through the tiny straw of her mixed drink.

"I bet you are," Rex laughed and sat up straight as the waitress brought his food.

Ask her what makes them so fun, a voice told him. The voice was so natural and real he thought for a minute he heard it audibly. He resisted the urge to scan over his shoulder to make sure nobody was behind him and had whispered in his ear. He chalked it up to being exhausted from the long day and took a bite of his lemongrass noodles.

"Bring him a beer," said Trisha to the waitress; Rex didn't understand what she said.

The waitress came right back with a cold, tall glass of beer and set it in front of Rex. He looked at it, then at Trisha. She was smiling and he saw mischief in her eyes.

"Fuck it!" Rex's two decades of sobriety came to an end. Simply put, his ego thought he could handle it, but the cunning, baffling and powerful grip of addiction, in an instant, swept him back to the gutter, like rubbish.

Rex picked up the glass and chugged the whole thing. He slammed the mug down, and wiped his chin with the back of his hand. The giggling girls heightened his already uncontrollable sexual urge.

"Waitress, three more drinks," he called out. "So, what kind of fun do you girls like to have?"

39

THE END

Exiting the airplane on his return from Thailand, Rex talked to himself the way he did before a race, *you can do this, it's been worse, hold it together,* as he walked down the Denver airport corridor, dreading having to see Bobby. The dark circles under his eyes and his sunken cheeks were telling of the choices he made while in Thailand.

Upon greeting Bobby, Rex saw the concerned gaze in his friend's eyes, "I'm exhausted. It was a long trip." Rex attributed his appearance to the grueling travel day. "But, man it's good to see you." The men hugged, Rex quickly backed off for fear Bobby would smell alcohol on him. "I just want to get home and go to sleep. I'll tell you all about my trip tomorrow."

"Let's get you home, there's no bed like your own bed," Bobby maintained his smile.

Ignoring his phone calls, Rex slept for two days. Shunning all his friends and all responsibilities, he paid attention to one thing: the taunting demons of his addiction back in full force. *See what you've been missing out on? This is who you are. You know you want it.* There was only one thing on his mind, and he knew right where to get it.

Triangle Park was the same; homeless people in ragged clothing were asleep on the benches, the lunch-line at the Rescue Mission turned onto the next street, and addicts loitered on every corner. Rex slowed and made eye contact with a tall, thin white man wearing a Broncos baseball cap. The man jerked his head, indicating where to meet.

"You a cop?" asked the dealer.

"No, man. Are you?"

"Fuck no. What can I do for you?"

"Got any H? A needle, too?" Rex flicked a fifty dollar bill.

The dealer pulled a small plastic baggy out of his pocket and kept it hidden in the palm of his hand. The exchange looked more like they were shaking hands than making an illegal transaction.

Rex drove off and found an unassuming place to park. With a sense of pride that he still possessed a knack for picking out the dealers, he dissolved some of the heroin and pulled it into the needle. His knuckles turned white from holding a tight fist until a vein bulged on the underside of his forearm. He released his hold and pumped his fist five times. The purple vein popped out as if it was lying on the top of his skin. He held the syringe in his right hand between his first and middle finger, and bent his wrist almost backward to point the needle toward the crease in his elbow, stuck it into his vein and injected himself. Euphoria washed over him like a soothing balm and made his head heavy causing it to fall back on the head-rest in his pick-up. His body felt warm and light like he was floating. The colors on the billboard up ahead glowed, vividly, and the model in the picture began to talk to him.

I've been waiting for you. I want to be with you. Do you want to be with me? Let's go sailing. Would you like that? He felt like he was inside the angelic sound and it was safe. Rex's head flopped to the side and drool ran down his chin. He tried to tell her yes, but his mouth wouldn't form the words. In his mind he was saying, yes, I want to go. I love you, but she couldn't hear him.

Rex forced his head back up so he could see the billboard. Her eyes glared at him and the large poster began to liquefy. *I'm going to kill you.* Her celestial voice now a bass tone with too much reverb. Rex's eyes rolled back and he passed out.

Hours later he returned home and checked his voice mail.

"Hey, it's Bobby, I'm worried about you. Hopefully, I'll see you at the meeting tonight. I know a lot of people want to hear about your trip, including me, still. I'm not sure why you're avoiding me. I hope my gut's wrong, it's telling me something's is very off. Give me a fucking call." Rex lowered his eyes and sighed. He deleted the message and went to bed guilt-ridden.

Awakened by the rising lump in his throat, Rex fell out of bed and crawled to the bathroom. He stuck his head in the toilet and vomited until everything was gone but the bile. The heaving caused his back to spasm and he collapsed on the pale blue linoleum floor. He lay there for half the day, too sick to move. During that time of agony, he recalled a poem he wrote years prior while in rehab. The words played over and over in his mind, like a skipping record of a little boy's voice.

The End

Rex, what happened? Where did you go?

You promised to take care of me and became my hero.

We flew together, you took me high and fast.

Up on the mountain you told me it would last.

Something befell and you didn't cope.

You threw me off the ledge and reached for your dope.

Don't you see my tears and the crack in my heart?

Please don't do this and rip us apart.

I'm begging you, just stop, this isn't OK.

I love you, I need you, don't float away.

Rex plugged his ears desperately wanting the poem to stop, he couldn't bear to listen to the haunting words. By the afternoon, in complete desperation, Rex changed, stuffed heroin and the needle into his pouch, and went to find what he knew would cure his ails.

It was a twenty-minute drive to East Colfax where prostitutes were readily available even in the afternoon. He picked up a hooker and they went to a motel room. This was his routine for the next week, as if he had never spent a sober day.

His addiction slinked its way back in, wrapped itself around his light and choked it out. The people he was around now, didn't notice his lifeless eyes, as they too displayed a battle weary thousand-yard stare. And, the demons kept seducing; *This is real living, all the pussy you want. You can't get this at a meeting. Where are those people now, anyway. Whose come over? All they do is call. They don't care about you, they never did.* He continued to avoid his recovery family and his obligations. His addiction had come back with a vengeance and snatched him out of the life he worked so hard for.

***

Plans of going to work as usual were interrupted, and instead, people were driving to Mile High Church to pay their respects. The mourners, some dressed in jeans and sweaters, others dressed in more formal attire walked briskly across the parking lot. It was 24 degrees with freezing drizzle on that gloomy Friday morning in early April as they entered the white dome-shaped building with a red brick-framed entrance. Just inside the glass doors, they were met by pictures of Rex and his infectious smile. A smile that normally brought a sense of warmth to the person receiving it, but not on that cold day. For some, emotions welled up right there in the foyer; for others, it wasn't until they uncomfortably took their seats in the unfamiliar hall that the weight of their grief crashed in on them. The reality that on

The End

March 27, 2007, two weeks after Rex returned home from Thailand, he was found dead in a seedy motel room in downtown Denver, an empty needle still in his arm.

That reality was almost incomprehensible.

"Hello, and welcome," the tall, slender, service officiate pushed his glasses up higher on his nose and addressed the mourners as pictures of Rex scrolled on the large screen behind the clergyman.

We are here today to honor and celebrate the life of Rex Sanford Patrick. I didn't know Rex that well, but I can tell by the standing room only crowd that he touched the lives of many people.

I know for many of you this is a very sad day, but we're here today to celebrate Rex's life and not to mourn it. Yes, that will come, however, for today, for this short time we're here together, let's put that aside and remember. With that, I would like to call up our first speaker. Come on up." The minister looked at Rex's long-time friend Jeff Schnaze and nodded.

"Hi, I'm Jeff."

"Hi Jeff," the audience responded.

"I've known Rex for about fifteen years, we met on the slopes. I'm also an amputee and Rex was my first ski instructor. Man, I don't know where to start, all of the shenanigans from that day. While riding up on the lift chair, if Rex saw an attractive girl he would yell 'hey blondie, shed the laundry.' He somehow

367

picked up on the fact that I was an addict and talked to me about spirituality, turning it into something cool and not religious. He showed me that day, that I could still have fun without being high and that was huge. After a few years, I got sober and we started mountain biking together.

I think with Rex, when he was on the mountain, he was there with God. That was his ultimate spiritual experience. He used to say, that for him, meditation was when he was on his bicycle. That was when he could feel the presence of God the most.

But, man, the demon that lives inside of us will come back to get us. No matter how much clean time you have, or how successful you become, if you put your recovery on the back burner, life can end.

It's profoundly sad, but he set another example for me. This time it was what not to do, and I have to thank him for that, too. It sounds bizarre, but for me, it's almost like a *Jesus* thing, like he died to help us remember how fragile our recovery is. Thanks for letting me talk."

"Thank you, Jeff, the minister shook his hand as they walked by each other on the platform. Our next person to come up is Bobby."

"Hi, I'm Bobby."

"Hi, Bobby."

The End

"Man, I hope I can get through this. I loved that guy like a brother." Bobby's voice cracked. "We were both cryers anyway, so it's fitting that I'm up here blubbering in front of you all."

The audience laughed, in need of a little comic relief. However, the sniffles of people crying could still be heard across the auditorium as Bobby continued.

"If it weren't so obvious, you would never know that Rex only had one leg, that guy could do anything. We were helping a friend build a room in his backyard and Rex dropped his crutches and climbed up to the top, sat on a beam and helped build the roof. I didn't even want to go up there.

Man, he always sported a smile, that guy could light up a room just by walking in. I don't think I've ever known someone so charismatic and determined. When he put his mind to do something, he didn't quit. Every time he came home with a new medal, my chest puffed up more than his. He always stayed humble.

I don't mountain bike, but man I loved it when I heard that he was called a billygoat. I can picture him riding up the side of a mountain like a madman. He'd get that crazed look in his eye and you knew to just get out of the way.

The guy just shined, his spirit would draw you to him. But, on the same hand, as Jeff said, he did have his demons.

There were things in his past that he just couldn't shake. It was weird to see two such extremes in the same human being. Knowing the tragedies he endured, I'm sure there was some irreparable damage to his soul. Which made him all that much more of an inspiration to me.

I tried so hard to talk him out of going to Thailand. He wouldn't listen. It just goes to show how cunning, baffling, and powerful this disease is. Rest in peace, my brother."

As Bobby walked off of the stage, the song Lean on Me, by Bill Withers, was playing. The audience silent and listening at first, slowly began to sing along. "Lean on me... I'll help you carry on." The lyrics resonated deeply as the voices got louder and louder until it resounded like an anthem throughout the sanctuary.

When the song ended, another person went up to speak as the more than five-hundred people listened and paid their respects.

"Hi, I'm Teresa."

"Hi, Teresa."

"Wow, I've never had that said back to me so loudly." Teresa fumbled with the microphone which caused a burst of screeching feedback. "Oh, sorry about that. I'm nervous."

"Anyway, I worked with Rex at the Community Care Center. He amazed me every time I saw him. He could fix anything and nothing was too small for him to bother with. One time I couldn't get the chair in my office to raise up, I felt so stupid. I called Rex to come and help me and he just flipped it upside down and fixed it. There was something wrong with a bolt or something. I didn't even ask. He sat in it and tested it out and said 'Mr. Fix-It strikes again raise it high and take a spin' and he spun around. He was funny and could just come up with the craziest stuff." Teresa swept her long brown curls off of her shoulders, then wiped her eyes with the tissue in her hand.

During all of the sharing time, the photo loop played in the background. A picture of Rex sitting by the fire with a group of friends at a campsite, all bundled up in his down jacket and beanie going cross-country skiing, sitting on his road bike with the mountains behind him, holding up his medals at a youth rally. The photos rolled by one by one and finally stopped on a close up of his face. The gleam in his eye, his sunkist cheeks and that bright smile hovered above the crowd almost life-like.

The minister came back up with some final words. " A f t e r talking with Rex's family, sitting here in the front row, these past few days and listening to the stories from people who loved Rex, one thing is very clear. Rex's bicycle was an extension of him. It was the place where he could release his aggression and experience a positive outcome."

The handsome man slipped his right hand into his pant pocket making his jacket bunch up behind his arm. He lowered his eyes and rubbed his shoe across the platform as if something was stuck on the floor.

"On his bike, that's where he bathed in a sense of peace, and where it felt that all was right with the world. Whether we address it or not, each of us has a *knowing* – the realization that we are a part of something bigger than ourselves. If we dare to embrace it … then in that space of time, when we let ourselves become fully submerged in it, we feel strangely safe.

It was on his bike where that state of grace, like a soft but firm blanket, wrapped itself around him and he felt protected. Rex carried the privilege of knowing that place. He understood its mystery.

One could anticipate his legacy would carry on to ignite all of us to dig deep and dream big. To trudge through the mire and turn our own vigor-stealing circumstances into triumphs. To be promoters of hope and vessels of encouragement.

The lessons we learn from Rex's life are the same lessons that come our way limitless times, and in a multitude of packages. To never take anything for granted. To live life to the fullest. To be fearless. To never give up. To be generous and kind. To be humble. To love.

I look at that picture and I am reminded that some souls just aren't meant to be contained."

THE END

About The Author

Lori built her foundation for healing through participating in the 12-step programs of Al-Anon and Adult Chidden of Alcoholics. She taught lessons in Bible-based Celebrate Recovery groups and shared her testimony with thousands of people. Lori developed her co-dependent skills as a pre-teen while the Patricks were part of her family. Rex and Lori were close during their teens, giving her much opportunity to hone her co-dependent mindset.

Lori received her BA in communications from CSU Hayward, where she wrote for the campus newspaper, The Pioneer, and was awarded for her contributing stories. She has written numerous short stories, short scripts, and poems. She caught her writing bug in elementary school when she was acknowledged for her creative story titled Glass House on a Shooting Star. It was when she received her God assignment that she began writing her debut novel Pushing Through.

Believing that everyone is recovering from something, as a transformational leader on Hawaii's Big Island, Lori helps people shift mindsets and recognize their inherent worth. Lori serves in church, works as a substitute teacher, and enjoys walks along the coast with her husband and two fur babies. Contact her on social media.

Early 1980; Rex, wearing prosthetic leg, braiding Lori's hair. Photo: Ann Courbot

1996 Atlanta Paralympics.
Photo: Mike Gladu

1981 Christmas
Photo: Ann Courbot

1992 Training in Barcelona
Photo: Jose Alcala

Made in the USA
Columbia, SC
23 January 2020